Library of Congress Control Number: 2013930756
Hardcover ISBN: 978-0-465-05872-3
E-book ISBN: 978-0-465-05870-9

10 9 8 7 6 5 4 3 2

INTELLECTUALS

AND RACE

THOMAS SOWELL

BASIC BOOKS

A Member of the Perseus Books Group
New York

The gods mercifully gave mankind this little moment of peace between the religious fanaticisms of the past and the fanaticisms of class and race that were speedily to arise and dominate time to come.

G.M. Trevelyan [1]

CONTENTS

INTRODUCTION

Intellectuals have had a powerful effect on racial and ethnic issues, in countries around the world, for at least the past hundred years— and there is no sign that their influence will not continue, for better or worse, in the generations ahead. Even within a given country, such as the United States, that influence has been exercised in diametrically opposite directions at different times, promoting racial segregation and eugenics in the early twentieth century, and then civil rights and affirmative action in the later decades of that century. In other countries and in different eras, intergroup differences have led to even more varied and extreme consequences, including outright civil war and mass murder.

Such issues and patterns will be explored in the chapters that follow. Most, but not all, of these chapters first appeared in a special section on race that was added to the revised edition of a much larger and more sweeping study, *Intellectuals and Society*. Here I have belatedly taken the advice of my research assistant Na Liu, and published these chapters in a separate book for those who wish to focus on racial issues, rather than take on the larger and more time-consuming task of traveling on a more sweeping journey across the landscape of intellectuals' influences on issues ranging from economics to law to war and peace.

New chapters have been added to this book, including the last chapter exploring current trends, in hopes of discerning their implications for the future. The chapters that precede this effort to foresee what lies ahead should tell us enough about what has already happened to make it obvious how large are the stakes and how difficult the choices facing this generation and those that will follow. If this book succeeds in simply demonstrating through its facts and analysis how inadequate, and even dangerous, the currently fashionable assumptions and catch phrases about race are, it will have achieved its purpose.

Chapter 1

Questions About Race

L ike many things that people are reluctant to discuss in polite society, or to discuss honestly, race is too important to be ignored or— worse yet— to think about only in the safe conventions and evasive phrases of our time. Too much of the history of race, in countries around the world, has been a story of hostility and hatred, and often a story written in blood. Ignorance about race is a luxury that few people of any race can afford. Misinformation is even worse, even when it is well-meaning misinformation.

The emotional difficulties of discussing race are matched by the intellectual difficulties. These difficulties begin with defining race itself. Ideally, we might think of a race as a set of people genetically and indelibly different from others in physical characteristics of one sort or another. But the ideal and the reality can differ as much when it comes to race as in any other aspect of human life. People have been singled out for racial discrimination, or even extermination, who looked so much like other members of the society in which they lived that they had to be forced to dress differently or to wear identifying insignia. Some have defined race broadly, such as black, white and yellow races, while others have considered Anglo-Saxons, Slavs and Celts to be different races. Racial intermixtures complicate definitions even more.*

Race is not entirely in the eye of the beholder, but it is a social concept with a biological basis. A stricter definition could lose touch with realities in societies where intermarriage is sharply increasing. Nor is intermarriage the ultimate solution to racial problems that many once thought. Jews in

---

* A white Congressman once said of black Congressman Augustus Hawkins, "Gus Hawkins is whiter than I am."

Germany in the 1920s had high rates of intermarriage,[1] but that did not stop the rise of Hitler in the 1930s or the Holocaust in the 1940s. Indeed, intermarriage led to larger numbers of offspring being classified as Jews, with tragic consequences. Arbitrary demarcations and inconsistent definitions of race have marked societies preoccupied with race, including the South of the Jim Crow era in the United States and white-ruled South Africa of the apartheid era.

Many have yearned for a society where race was irrelevant, and some saw the election of the first black President of the United States as a major step toward that kind of society. But polls on support for, and opposition to, that president among different ethnic groups are just one sign of continuing racial polarization. In short, no matter how ultimately irrelevant race may seem to some, racial issues show no sign of going away. They cannot be ignored. The only question is how we confront them.

That is a special question when it comes to intellectuals, because their views can influence the way millions of other people see race, as the tendencies, preconceptions and conclusions of the intelligentsia spread through the media and educational institutions from the schools to the universities. For better or worse, intellectuals have played a large role in racial issues in many countries around the world. In the United States, they have played opposite roles on racial issues in the early twentieth century as contrasted with the late twentieth century. These roles and these issues are explored in the chapters that follow, leading to many conclusions very different from those currently prevailing in the media, in politics or in academia.

Both "intellectuals" and "race" are words with many elusive definitions. By "intellectuals" is meant here people in a particular occupation— namely, people whose work begins and ends with ideas. It is an occupational designation, rather than an honorific title, and implies nothing about the mental level of those in that occupation. Chemists or chess grandmasters may be of equal or greater mental accomplishment, but they are not intellectuals because their work ends with an outcome subject to empirical verification by known standards, while the outcomes of the work of intellectuals are subject essentially to peer consensus. Even in academia, professors of medicine or engineering are not what come to mind when intellectuals are discussed, even though they may be the mental equals or superiors of professors of sociology or literature.

These are not just verbal issues about nomenclature. Any attempt to have rational discourse requires that those with different views have a common language in which to discuss their differences. And there is no subject more in need of rational discourse than is the subject of race.

While Americans are rightly concerned about issues involving racial and ethnic groups in their own country, such issues are common in other societies around the world. Moreover, even to understand what is happening in one country may require some knowledge of the extent to which similar things have been present in other societies, and whether they have led to similar or different outcomes.

This is especially so when a given outcome in one country is attributed to a given factor— and yet that same outcome can be found in other countries where that factor is absent. For example, when lower class whites in Britain exhibit strikingly similar behavior patterns to those of blacks in America, attributing those behavior patterns among American blacks to "a legacy of slavery" or to past or contemporary racial discrimination, is offering an explanation which obviously cannot apply to lower class Britons who have experienced neither. That then calls into question to what extent it applies to American blacks, though many take such explanations as a foregone conclusion requiring no further inquiry or closer scrutiny.

Much that has been said on many sides of racial and ethnic issues requires far more inquiry and far closer scrutiny than that behind currently prevailing views. This book attempts to provide some of that further inquiry and closer scrutiny.

E. Franklin Frazier urged that the history of black Americans be studied in a larger, international context.[2] In the chapters that follow, American racial and ethnic issues in general will be put in an international context. This neither assumes nor denies the uniqueness of American racial and ethnic issues, but lets that be an empirical question.

There is no subject that is more in need of dispassionate analysis, careful factual research and a fearless and honest discussion than is race. Ideally, we might look to intellectuals for such things. But it is also true that the mental skills and verbal dexterity of intellectuals can be used to evade evidence and promote whatever beliefs or agendas are in vogue among their peers. The intelligentsia in the media can decide what to emphasize, what to downplay and what to ignore entirely when it comes to race. These may be individual choices, rather than a conspiracy, but individual choices growing out of a common vision of the world can produce results all too similar to what is produced by centralized censorship or propaganda.

As a concrete example, statistics comparing American blacks and whites in many respects— jobs, incomes, and mortgage approval rates, for example— are often drawn from data that include similar information about Asian Americans. Yet seldom are the Asian American data included in news stories, or even in academic studies, which conclude that racial discrimination explains much or most of the disparities between blacks and whites. In many, if not most, cases, reporting the data for Asian Americans would undermine, if not devastate, the conclusions reached from black-white comparisons.

In the job market, for example, it has often been said over the years that blacks are "the last hired and the first fired," since black employees are often terminated during an economic downturn sooner or to a greater extent than white employees. Data thus seem to substantiate this social vision of the world common among the intelligentsia and others. But if data on Asian Americans were included— which seldom happens— it would turn out that white employees are usually let go before Asian American employees.[3] Can this be attributed to racial discrimination against whites by employers who are usually white themselves? More fundamentally, can we accept statistical data as showing discrimination in cases where that reinforces existing preconceptions, and then reject the same kind of data when it goes counter to those preconceptions?

It is much the same story when examining what happens to people who apply for mortgage loans. There has been much indignant outcry in the media when statistics have shown that black applicants for mortgage loans were turned down more often than white applicants. Newspapers across the country, as well as television commentators, have treated such statistics as proof of racial discrimination by white banks against black applicants for mortgage loans. Yet statistical data on Asian Americans have been conspicuous by their absence from these comparisons as well. If such data are included, it turns out that, in 2000, black applicants were turned down for prime mortgage loans twice as often as white applicants— and white applicants were turned down nearly twice as often as Asian American applicants.[4]

The question arises again whether we are going to accept statistical data as evidence of racial discrimination when it fits the preconceptions of the intelligentsia and reject it when it goes counter to those preconceptions. In the case of mortgage loans, there is other evidence against the conclusions reached almost universally in the media and in academia. Average credit scores are higher among whites than among blacks— and higher among Asian Americans than among whites.[5] Taking into account the data for Asian Americans threatens to reduce a moral melodrama to a mundane matter of elementary economics in which lenders are more likely to lend to people who are more likely to pay them back.

Since many, if not most, of those financial officials who actually make the decision to lend, or not to lend, do so on the basis of paperwork passed on to them from others who do the face to face interviews with applicants, it is doubtful whether these decision-making officials even know the race of the applicants. But differences in credit scores and other qualifications virtually guarantee racial disparities in outcomes anyway. Again, it seems hardly likely that white-owned banks are discriminating against whites and in favor of Asian Americans. Moreover, black-owned banks turn down black mortgage loan applicants at an even higher rate than do white-owned banks,[6] and it seems equally unlikely that this is due to racial discrimination.

It is much the same story in the public schools, where black students are disciplined for misbehavior more often than white students— who in turn are disciplined more often than Asian American students.[7] Again, the question must be faced whether disparities in outcomes represent disparities in behavior or disparities in the way that others treat various races. Certainly the disparities themselves cannot be denied, however much different observers may attribute these disparities to very different causes. This extends far beyond questions of blacks and whites in the United States because, as we shall see, disparities of similar or greater magnitude are common in other countries around the world.

Uncritical use of statistics risks many pitfalls. The very definitions used with statistical data create traps for the unwary. For example, when the Ravenswood School District in California turned out to have the country's highest rate of disciplining of students who are "Asian and Pacific Islanders,"[8] that was taken by some as showing racial discrimination. However, the omnibus category "Asian and Pacific Islanders" includes many very different groups. People whose ancestors originated in China, India or Japan are very different in many ways from people who originated in Guam or Samoa. In most places in the United States, most of the "Asian and Pacific Islanders" are people from the mainland of Asia. But, in the Ravenswood School District, most of the students who are "Asian and Pacific Islanders" are the offspring of Pacific Islanders.[9] Comparisons of outcomes in this school district with outcomes in other school districts across the country are comparisons of apples and oranges.

This small example is a microcosm of problems involved in attempting to understand racial and ethnic issues, whether these issues are expressed in numbers or in words, and whether they are expressed by the intelligentsia, the media or academia.

Chapter 2

Disparities and
Their Causes

Any serious study of racial and ethnic groups, whether in a given society or in a wide variety of societies in countries around the world, repeatedly encounters the inescapable fact of large and numerous disparities among these groups, whether in income, education, crime rates, IQs or many other things. These differences cannot be dismissed as mere "perceptions" or "stereotypes," nor can they be automatically attributed to some one given cause, such as genetics, as was often the primary cause cited in the early twentieth century, or to maltreatment by others, as was equally often cited in the late twentieth century.

The sources of these disparities are numerous and complex, and they must be confronted in their complexity, if we are seeking the truth, rather than trying to promote a vision or an agenda.

THE REALITY OF DISPARITIES

Sometimes minorities are on the short end of disparities (as in the United States, Britain and France), and sometimes it is a majority that lags behind (as in Malaysia, Indonesia or the Ottoman Empire). Sometimes the disparities are blamed on discrimination, sometimes on genes, but in any event the disparities are treated as oddities that need explaining, *no matter how common such supposed oddities are in countries around the world* or in how many centuries they have been common. Because intellectuals' assumptions about these disparities are so deeply ingrained, so widely disseminated, and

7

have such powerful ramifications on so many issues, it is worth taking a closer and longer look at the facts of the real world, now and in the past.

Where minorities have outperformed politically dominant majorities, it is especially difficult to make the case that discrimination is the cause.* A study of the Ottoman Empire, for example, found that "of the 40 private bankers listed in Istanbul in 1912 not one bore a Muslim name." Nor was even one of the 34 stockbrokers in Istanbul a Turk. Of the capital assets of 284 industrial firms employing five or more workers, 50 percent were owned by Greeks and another 20 percent by Armenians.[1] In the seventeenth century Ottoman Empire, the palace medical staff consisted of 41 Jews and 21 Muslims.[2]

The racial or ethnic minorities who have owned or directed more than half of whole industries in particular nations have included the Chinese in Malaysia,[3] the Lebanese in West Africa,[4] Greeks in the Ottoman Empire,[5] Britons in Argentina,[6] Belgians in Russia,[7] Jews in Poland,[8] and Spaniards in Chile[9]— among many others. As of 1921, members of the Tamil minority in Ceylon outnumbered members of the Sinhalese majority in that country's medical profession.[10] In America, there were eight times during the twentieth century when a baseball player stole 100 or more bases in a season; all eight times that player was black.[11]

Groups have differed greatly in innumerable endeavors in countries around the world. In 1908, Germans were the sole producers of the following products in Brazil's state of São Paulo: metal furniture, trunks, stoves, paper, hats, neckties, leather, soap, glass, matches, beer, confections, and carriages.[12] People of Japanese ancestry who settled in that same state produced more than two-thirds of the potatoes and more than 90 percent of the tomatoes.[13] Exporters from the Lebanese minority in the African nation of Sierra Leone accounted for 85 percent of the exports of ginger in 1954 and 93 percent in 1955.[14] In 1949, Lebanese truckers in Sierra Leone outnumbered African truckers and European truckers combined.[15]

In 1921, more than three-fifths of all the commerce in Poland was conducted by Jews, who were only 11 percent of the population.[16] In 1948,

---

* The problems with genetics as an all-purpose explanation will be dealt with in the next chapter.

members of the Indian minority owned roughly nine-tenths of all the cotton gins in Uganda.[17] In colonial Ceylon, the textile, retailing, wholesaling, and import businesses were all largely in the hands of people of Indian ancestry, rather than in the hands of the Sinhalese majority.[18]

As early as 1887, more than twice as many Italians as Argentines had bank accounts in the *Banco de la Provincia de Buenos Aires*,[19] even though most nineteenth-century Italian immigrants arrived in Argentina destitute and began working in the lowest, hardest, and most "menial" jobs. In the United States, knowledge of the frugality of Italian immigrants, and their reliability in repaying debts, even when they had low incomes, caused a bank to be set up to attract this clientele in San Francisco, under the name "Bank of Italy." It became so successful that it spread out to the larger society, and eventually became the largest bank in the world under its new name, "Bank of America."[20] The frugality of Italians was not simply a "perception" or a "stereotype," as A.P. Giannini well knew when he set up this bank. As far away as Australia, Italians "earned a reputation for scrupulous honesty in the repayment of their debts, and were frequently able to secure more extensive loans than Australians."[21]

At one period of history or another, when it was not one specific racial or ethnic minority dominating an industry or occupation, it has often been foreigners in general, leaving the majority population of a country outnumbered, or even non-existent, in whole sectors of their own economy. Even after the middle of the twentieth century, most of the industrial enterprises in Chile were controlled by either immigrants or the children of immigrants.[22] At various times and places, foreign minorities have predominated in particular industries or occupations over the majority populations of Peru,[23] Switzerland,[24] Malaysia,[25] Argentina,[26] Russia,[27] much of the Balkans,[28] the Middle East,[29] and Southeast Asia.[30] Indeed, it has been a worldwide phenomenon, found even in some economically advanced countries, as well as being common in less advanced countries.

In the nineteenth century, Scottish highlanders were not as prosperous as Scottish lowlanders, whether in Scotland itself or as immigrants living in Australia or the United States.[31] In the twentieth century, Gaelic-speaking children in the Hebrides Islands off Scotland did not score as high on IQ tests as the English-speaking children there.[32] Rates of alcoholism among Irish-Americans have at one time been some multiple of the rates of alcoholism among Italian Americans or Jewish Americans.[33] In the days of the Soviet Union, the consumption of cognac in Estonia was more than seven times what it was in Uzbekistan.[34] In Malaysia during the 1960s, students from the Chinese minority earned more than 400 degrees in engineering, while students from the Malay majority earned just four engineering degrees during that same decade.[35]

Such examples could be extended almost indefinitely,* and so could the reasons for the disparities. But a more fundamental question must be faced: Was there ever any realistic chance that the various races would have had the same skills, experience and general capabilities, even if they had the same genetic potential and faced no discrimination?

FACTORS BEHIND DISPARITIES

Different races, after all, developed in different parts of the world, in very different geographic settings, which presented very different opportunities and restrictions on their economic and cultural evolution over a period of centuries.

There is no way, for example, that the patterns of economic and social life which originated and evolved in Europe could have originated among the

---

* For example, a study of military forces in countries around the world found that "militaries fall far short of mirroring, even roughly, the multi-ethnic societies" from which they come. Cynthia H. Enloe, *Police, Military and Ethnicity: Foundations of State Power* (New Brunswick: Transaction Books, 1980), p. 143. Another massive scholarly study of ethnic groups in countries around the world concluded that, when discussing "proportional representation" of ethnic groups, "few, if any, societies have ever approximated this description." Donald L. Horowitz, *Ethnic Groups in Conflict* (Berkeley: University of California Press, 1985), p. 677. Yet another such international study of ethnic groups referred to "the universality of ethnic inequality" and pointed out that these inequalities are multi-dimensional: "All multi-ethnic societies exhibit a tendency for ethnic groups to engage in different occupations, have different levels (and, often, types) of education, receive different incomes, and occupy a different place in the social hierarchy." Myron Weiner, "The Pursuit of Ethnic Equality through Preferential Policies: A Comparative Public Policy Perspective," *From Independence to Statehood*, edited by Robert B. Goldmann and A. Jeyaratnam Wilson (London: Frances Pinter, 1984), p. 64.

indigenous peoples of the Western Hemisphere, where the horses that were central to everything from farming to transportation to warfare in Europe simply did not exist anywhere in the Western Hemisphere when the European invaders arrived and began transplanting horses across the Atlantic to the New World. Take horses out of the history of Europe and a very different kind of economy and society would have had to evolve, in order to be viable. Not only horses were lacking in the Western Hemisphere, neither were there oxen, which were common in both Europe and Asia. There were, in short, no such heavy-duty beasts of burden in the Western Hemisphere as existed on the vast Eurasian land mass, where most of the human race has lived throughout recorded history. The way of life in these different regions of the world had no basis on which to be the same— which is to say, there was no way for the skills and experiences of the races in these regions to be the same.

The wheel has often been regarded as fundamental to economic and social advances but, for most of the history of the human race, the value of wheeled vehicles depended to a great extent on the presence of draft animals to pull those vehicles— and there were no wheeled vehicles in any of the economies of the Western Hemisphere when the Europeans arrived. The Mayans had invented wheels, but they were used on children's toys,[36] so the issue was not the intellectual capacity to invent the wheel but the circumstances that make wheels more valuable or less valuable. Clearly, the way of life among the indigenous peoples of the Western Hemisphere could not have been the same as that on the Eurasian land mass, when there were neither wheeled vehicles nor draft animals in the Western Hemisphere when the Europeans and their animals arrived. Regardless of which race lived in Europe or in the Western Hemisphere, they would have faced very different opportunities or restrictions as regards their economic and cultural development before they encountered each other, and could hardly have been the same at that time.

Geographic differences between Europe and sub-Saharan Africa are even more numerous and more drastic than those between Europe and the Western Hemisphere.[37] In addition to severe geographic limitations on the production of wealth, due to deficiencies of soil and unreliable rainfall patterns,[38] sub-Saharan Africa has had severe geographic restrictions on communications among its own fragmented peoples, and of these peoples with the peoples of the outside world, due to a dearth of navigable waterways within sub-Saharan Africa, as well as a dearth of natural harbors, the difficulties of maintaining draft animals because of the disease-carrying tsetse fly, and the vast barrier of the Sahara desert, which is several times the size of any other desert in the world, and as large as the 48 contiguous states of the United States. With an expanse of sand that size standing between them and the outside world to the north, and with three oceans on the other sides of them, the peoples of sub-Saharan Africa have long been among the most insulated from the rest of the human race.

Isolated peoples in many parts of the world have for centuries lagged behind others, whether the isolation has been caused by mountains, deserts, or islands far from the nearest mainland. Eminent French historian Fernand Braudel pointed out, "mountain life persistently lagged behind the plain."[39] The inhabitants of the Canary Islands were people of a Caucasian race who were living at a stone-age level when they were discovered by the Spaniards in the fifteenth century.[40] On the other side of the world, the similarly isolated Australian aborigines similarly lagged far behind the progress of the outside world.[41] Sub-Saharan Africans have been part of a worldwide pattern of isolated peoples lagging behind others in technology, organization and in other ways.

In addition to having many geographic barriers limiting their access to the peoples and cultures of other lands, sub-Saharan Africans also faced internal geographic barriers limiting their access to each other. The resulting internal cultural fragmentation is indicated by the fact that, while Africans are only about ten percent of the world's population, they have one-third of the world's languages.[42]

Eventually, the severe isolation of many sub-Saharan Africans was ended in the modern era, as that of other severely isolated peoples was ended, but that was after millennia in which these isolated peoples had developed whole ways of life very different from the ways of life that developed among those peoples of Europe and Asia who had far greater access to a far wider cultural universe. Moreover, cultures— whole ways of life— do not simply evaporate when conditions change, whether among Africans or others.

Long-standing and deep-seated cultural differences can become cultural barriers, even after the geographic barriers that created cultural isolation have been overcome with the growth of modern transportation and communication. As distinguished cultural historian Oscar Handlin put it: "men are not blank tablets upon which the environment inscribes a culture which can readily be erased to make way for a new inscription."[43] As another noted historian put it: "We do not live in the past, but the past in us."[44]

Even the geographic differences between Eastern Europe and Western Europe[45] have left the peoples of Eastern Europe with a lower standard of living than that of Western Europeans for centuries, including in our own times a larger economic disparity between the people in these two regions of Europe than the per capita income disparity between blacks and whites in the United States.[46] As Professor Angelo Codevilla of Boston University put it, "a European child will have a very different life depending on whether that baby was born east or west of a line that starts at the Baltics and stretches southward along Poland's eastern border, down Slovakia's western border and along the eastern border of Hungary, then continues down through the middle of Bosnia to the Adriatic Sea."[47] Both geography and history have for centuries presented very different opportunities to people born east and west of that line.[48]

In addition to the inherent geographic advantages that Western Europe has had over Eastern Europe— for example, more navigable waterways leading to the open seas, with Western European rivers and harbors not being frozen over as often or as long in winter as rivers and harbors in Eastern Europe, due to the warming effect of the Gulf Stream on Western Europe— another major historic advantage growing out of geography is that Western Europe was more readily accessible to invasion by Roman conquerors. Despite the ruthless slaughters in those conquests and the subsequent brutal oppressions by the Roman overlords, among the lasting advantages which the Roman conquests brought to Western Europe were Roman letters, so that Western European languages had written versions, centuries before the languages of Eastern Europe did.

To the enormous advantages of literacy, as such, Western Europeans had the further advantage of a far greater accumulation of written knowledge in their languages, even after the languages of Eastern Europe began to develop written versions, but still had not yet caught up with the centuries-long accumulations of knowledge written in Western European languages.

Literacy was not the only thing that moved from west to east in Europe. So did coins, printing presses, castles, crossbows, paved streets, and vaccinations, among other economic and social advances. But all of this took time, sometimes centuries. Moreover, people from Western Europe— Germans, Jews and others— were often a majority of the population in Eastern European cities in earlier centuries, while Slavs remained a huge majority in the surrounding countrysides. For example, before 1312 the official records of the city of Cracow were kept in German— and the transition, at that point, was to Latin. Only decades later did Poles become a majority of the population in Cracow.[49] The towns of medieval East Central Europe were often cultural enclaves of foreigners— again, mostly Germans, but with many Jews as well and, in the Balkans, Greeks and Armenians, joined in later centuries by Turks.[50]

In short, there has been for centuries, not only a disparity between the opportunities and advances in the two halves of Europe, but great disparities within Eastern Europe itself between the indigenous peoples of the region and the transplanted Western Europeans living in Eastern Europe, the Baltic and the Balkans. Neither genes nor discrimination are necessary to explain this situation, though some intellectuals and politicians have chosen to claim that the differences have been due to race and others have chosen to blame social injustices. Many other racial and other groups in many other parts of the world have likewise ended up with large disparities in opportunities and achievements, for reasons that range across a wide spectrum and cannot be reduced to genes or injustices.

How could people living in the Himalayas develop the seafaring skills of people living in ports around the Mediterranean? How could the Bedouins of the Sahara know as much about fishing as the Polynesians of the Pacific— or the Polynesians know as much about camels as the Bedouins? How could Eskimos be as proficient at growing tropical crops as the people of Hawaii or the Caribbean?

Such considerations are far more crucial for practical knowledge than for academic knowledge. Ph.D.s in mathematics can have the same knowledge in Delhi as in Paris. However, in the world of mundane but consequential knowledge, how could an industrial revolution have originated in places which lack the key natural resources— iron ore and coal— and are too geographically inaccessible for those resources to be transported to them without prohibitive costs? The industrial revolution could hardly have begun in the Balkans or Hawaii, regardless of what people were living there— *and neither could the people in those places have developed the same industrial skills, habits and ways of life* at the same time as people in other places where the industrial revolution did in fact begin.

There is no need to replace genetic determinism with geographic determinism. While there are other factors which operate against the presumed equality of developed capabilities among people with equal potential, the point here is that geography alone is enough to prevent equality of developed capabilities, even if all races have identical potentialities and there is no discrimination. Nor is it necessary to determine the relative weights of geographic, demographic, cultural and other factors, when the more fundamental point is that each of these factors makes equal outcomes among races, classes or other subdivisions of the human species progressively less likely.

Among the many different groups in countries around the world, very few have ever matched the major role played by the Jains from India in the cutting of diamonds for the world market, whether the Jains lived in India or in Amsterdam. People of German ancestry have been similarly prominent in the brewing of beer, whether in Germany or in the United States, where the best-selling brands of beer were created by people of German ancestry, as was true of China's famous Tsingtao beer. In nineteenth century Argentina, German beer drove English ale from the local market, while Germans also established breweries in Australia and Brazil, as they had brewed beer in the days of the Roman Empire.

Jews have been similarly prominent, if not predominant, in the apparel industry, whether in medieval Spain, the Ottoman Empire, Eastern Europe, Argentina or the United States. Yet intellectuals' emphasis on external circumstances over internal cultures led an academic historian to say that Jewish immigrants to the United States were fortunate that they arrived in this country just when the garment industry was about to take off.[51] The same coincidence seems to have occurred in a number of other countries, just as the arrival of large numbers of overseas Chinese in various countries in Southeast Asia galvanized particular sectors of the economies there, and the arrival of the Huguenots galvanized the watch-making industry in seventeenth-century England.

In addition to intergroup differences in particular occupational skills, there are large and consequential differences in median age. Some groups differ by a decade in median age and others differ by two decades or more.[52] Large differences among groups in median age occur both within nations and between nations. Just among Asian Americans, the median age ranges from 43 years old for Japanese Americans to 24 years old for Americans of Cambodian ancestry.[53] Among nations, the median age in Germany and Japan is over forty, while the median age in Afghanistan and Yemen is under twenty.[54] How a group of people, whether races or nations, whose median ages are decades apart could have the same knowledge, skills and experience— or have the same outcomes that depend on such knowledge, skills and experience— is a question that need not be faced by those who proceed as if disparities in outcomes must indicate differences in genes or discrimination, rather than numerous other factors that create disparities in inputs.

Historical happenstances— the fact that certain decisive military battles could easily have gone the other way, and changed the future of whole nations and races— are among those other factors. Had the battle of Tours in 732 or the siege of Vienna in 1529 gone the other way, this could be a very different world today. But these other factors besides geography tend to remove equal developed capabilities even further from the realm of reality.

Since the geography of the planet is not something "socially constructed," the misfortunes of lagging groups are not automatically a *social* injustice, even if they can be conceived of as injustices from some cosmic perspective, in the sense that many peoples have suffered serious deprivations through no fault of their own. Putting the onus on society by calling these deprivations a violation of "social justice" may be a verbal sop to those who are lagging, but it points them away from the paths by which other lagging groups have advanced themselves in the past, by pointing them toward blaming other people.

Cultural attitudes, which in some societies create a rigid division between "women's work" and "men's work," or which make manual labor repugnant to people with education, or caste-ridden societies which drastically limit the sources from which particular talents can be drawn for accomplishing particular tasks, all affect the economic potential of a given society. A society which throws away the talents and potentialities of half its population by making many economic roles and endeavors off-limits to women can hardly be expected to match the economic performances of societies which do not restrict their own prospects like this. In a society with rigid class or caste divisions, the highly varied talents and potentialities which arise among individuals may not arise solely, or even predominantly, among those individuals who happen to be born within the rigid class or caste stratifications in which their talents and potentialities are considered appropriate, or in which those talents and potentialities have opportunities to reach fruition.

These are among the many reasons why societies, races and civilizations are extremely unlikely to have identical achievements, even in the complete absence of genetic deficiencies or social injustices.

What does all this boil down to?

1. Grossly uneven distributions of racial, ethnic and other groups in numerous fields of endeavor have been common in countries around the world and for centuries of recorded history.
2. The even, proportional or statistically random distribution of these groups, which has been taken as a norm, deviations from which have been regarded as evidence of either genetic differences in ability (in the early 20th century) or as evidence of maltreatment by others (in the late 20th century) has seldom, if ever, been demonstrated empirically, or even been asked to be demonstrated.

The disparity in burdens of proof for different beliefs about the causes of inequality of outcomes rivals the disparities in these outcomes themselves. Not only in the American media and popular discourse, but in academic institutions and in courts of law— all the way up to the Supreme Court of the United States— *no burden of proof whatever* is required for the presumption that disparate outcomes at a given institution constitute *prima facie* evidence of discrimination at that institution, which legally shifts the burden of proof of innocence to the accused, contrary to legal traditions in other contexts, where it is the accuser who has the burden of proof, whether in criminal or civil cases.

BEHAVIOR AND BELIEFS

Not only do different racial, ethnic, and other groups differ in their occupational skills and experience, they tend also to differ in their beliefs and behavior toward other groups and internally among themselves.

Reluctance to associate with any group, whether at work or in neighborhood or other settings, is almost automatically attributed by the intelligentsia to ignorance, prejudice or malice— in utter disregard of not only the first-hand experience of those who are reluctant, but also of objective data on vast differences in rates of crime, alcoholism, and substandard school performances between groups, even though such differences have been common in countries around the world for centuries.

Cholera, for example, was unknown in America until large numbers of Irish immigrants arrived in the nineteenth century, and cholera outbreaks in New York and Philadelphia went largely through Irish neighborhoods.[55] People who did not want to live near Irish immigrants, as a result of diseases, violence and other social pathology rampant in the Irish communities of that era, cannot be automatically dismissed as blinded by prejudice or deceived by stereotypes.* Strenuous efforts, especially by the Catholic Church, to change the behavior patterns within Irish American communities,[56] suggest that it was not all a matter of other people's "perceptions" or "stereotypes." Moreover, these efforts within Irish American

---

* "The Germans in St. Louis were principally concentrated in the northern and southern sections of the city. The Irish also had their own special area, and it was never safe to venture from one section into the other... Rioting occurred also when Irish rowdies interfered with German picnics, frequently for no apparent reason except to add excitement to an otherwise dull Sunday." Carl Wittke, *The Irish in America* (New York: Russell & Russell, 1970), p. 183.

communities ultimately paid off, as barriers against the Irish, epitomized by employers' signs that said "No Irish Need Apply," faded away over the generations.

Such barriers were not simply a matter of mistaken or malign ideas in other people's heads, nor were the Irish simply abstract people in an abstract world, however much that vision may flatter intellectuals' desires to be on the side of the angels against the forces of evil. There is no need to go to the opposite extreme and claim that *all* negative views of all groups are based on valid reasons. The point here is that this is an empirical question to be investigated in terms of the particular facts of the particular group at a particular time and place— a process circumvented by reasoning as if discussing abstract people in an abstract world.

People sort themselves out in innumerable ways, both between races and within races, as well as in situations where race is not a salient factor. For example, studies have shown the correlation between the IQs of husbands and their wives to be similar to— and sometimes greater than— the correlation between the IQs of brothers and sisters,[57] even though there is no genetic or biological reason for spouses to be similar in IQ. Only the fact that people behave differently toward people whom they perceive as similar to themselves seems likely to explain IQ correlations between people who get married, even though they do not give IQ tests to one another before deciding to wed.

It is easy to tell when different racial and ethnic groups live separately when these groups have physical differences that are visible to the naked eye— blacks and whites being an obvious example. However, such residential differences are common in countries around the world, even when there are no physical differences to catch the eye of observers.

As late as the second half of the twentieth century, if one wished to have Americans of northern European ancestry and Americans of southern European ancestry living randomly distributed with one another in the New York metropolitan area, it would be necessary to move just over half of all Americans of southern European ancestry.[58] At the beginning of the twentieth century, when Jewish immigrants and their children were concentrated on the Lower East Side of Manhattan, they were not randomly distributed; Hungarian Jews were clustered together, as were

Polish, Rumanian and other Jews.[59] Meanwhile, German Jews lived uptown. In Chicago, when Eastern European Jews began moving into German Jewish neighborhoods, German Jews began moving out.[60]

It was much the same story among blacks in Chicago. Sociological studies by E. Franklin Frazier in the 1930s found different classes of blacks living in different parts of Chicago's black community. Some black neighborhoods in Chicago had delinquency rates over 40 percent and others had delinquency rates under 2 percent.[61] Meanwhile, in Harlem during the same era, "Observant subway riders could see the porters and domestics get off at West 125th Street, the clerks and secretaries depart at West 135th Street, and the doctors and lawyers leave at West 145th Street."[62]

In Italian East Harlem, people from Genoa lived clustered together and separate from the clusters of Italians from Naples or Sicily.[63] Similar regional clusters of Italians existed on New York's Lower East side, as well as in San Francisco, Cleveland, New Haven and other American cities.[64] None of this was peculiar to the United States. Similar clusters of Italians from particular places in Italy were also common in Buenos Aires and Toronto during the immigrant era.[65]

Considering an opposite approach may make the difference between reasoning in the abstract and reasoning in the concrete stand out more sharply. When a scholarly study of economic development in Latin America concluded, "Costa Rica is different from Nicaragua *because Costa Ricans are different from Nicaraguans*,"[66] its conclusion— whatever its merits or demerits— was one almost unthinkable within the confines of the vision prevailing among intellectuals today, even as a hypothesis to be tested. The opposite approach— treating Costa Ricans and Nicaraguans as if they were abstract people in an abstract world, whose differences in outcomes could only be a result of external circumstances— has been far more common among the intelligentsia.

Chapter 3

Changing Racial Beliefs

For centuries, there have been beliefs that some races are superior to others. Various developments in the second half of the nineteenth century, and in the early twentieth century, turned such general beliefs into organized ideologies with the aura of "science," often creating the very dogmatism among intellectuals that science is meant to counter. By the end of the twentieth century, opposite ideologies about race would prevail among intellectuals, sometimes also invoking the name of science, with no more justification and with the same dismissive attitude toward those who dared to disagree with the currently prevailing vision.

The term "race," as it was used in the late nineteenth and early twentieth centuries, was not confined to broad divisions of the human species, such as black, white and yellow races. Differences among Slavs, Jews and Anglo-Saxons were often referred to as "racial" differences as well. Madison Grant's influential 1916 best-seller, *The Passing of the Great Race*, was one of those writings which divided Europeans into Nordic, Alpine and Mediterranean "races," among others.[1]

Rather than become bogged down in semantic issues, we can refer to racial and ethnic groups loosely under the rubric of race, in part because more precise definitions could easily lose touch with social realities, in a world of growing racial intermixtures over the generations. These biological intermixtures have accelerated in our own times, even as the stridency of separate racial identity rhetoric has increased. These include people bitterly complaining about how half their ancestors mistreated the other half, as a current grievance of their own, whether among the Maoris of New Zealand or among various American racial or ethnic groups.

With race, as with war, twentieth century intellectuals were concentrated on one end of the spectrum in the early years and then on the opposite end of the spectrum in later years. The prevailing over-arching vision among intellectuals— that is, a preference for a society guided from the top down by ideas inspired by intellectual elites— was the same at the beginning and end of that century. But this general preference need not require a commitment to a particular view of a particular issue such as race, even though whatever view happened to prevail among the intelligentsia at a given time was often deemed to be almost axiomatically superior to conflicting views held by others— these other views often being treated as unworthy of serious intellectual engagement. In the early twentieth century, Madison Grant referred to those who disagreed with his genetic determinism as sentimentalists[2] and, in the late twentieth century, those who disagreed with the prevailing racial orthodoxy of that era were often dismissed as racists.

Intellectuals on opposite ends of the spectrum in different eras have been similar in another way: Both have tended to ignore the long-standing warning from statisticians that correlation is not causation. One race may be more successful than another at a particular endeavor, or a whole range of endeavors, for reasons that are neither genetic nor a result of the way the society in which they live treats them. As noted in Chapter 2, there are many historic, geographic and demographic reasons for groups to differ from one another in their skills, experiences, cultures and values— whether these are different social, national or racial groups.

GENETIC DETERMINISM

The mid-nineteenth century sensation created by Charles Darwin's theory of evolution had ramifications far beyond the field of biology. The idea of "survival of the fittest" among competing species was extended by others into competition among human beings, whether among different classes or different races. The research of Darwin's cousin Francis Galton (1822–1911) culminated in a book titled *Hereditary Genius*, which established that high achievers were concentrated in particular families.

Correlation was treated as causation, with genetics being proclaimed to be the reason for the achievement differential.

Similar reasoning was applied to races. As a later scholar said of Galton: "He believed that in his own day the Anglo-Saxons far outranked the Negroes of Africa, who in turn outranked the Australian aborigines, who outranked nobody." Again, correlation was treated as causation, leading to eugenics— a term Galton coined— to promote the differential survival of races. He said, "there exists a sentiment, for the most part quite unreasonable, against the gradual extinction of an inferior race."[3]

Whatever the validity of Galton's assessments of the relative achievements of different races in his own time, profound changes in the relative achievements of different races over the centuries undermine the theory of genetic determinism. China was, for centuries, technologically, economically, and in other ways more advanced than any country in Europe. The later reversals of the relative positions of the Chinese and Europeans in the modern era, without any demonstrable changes in their genes, undermine Galton's genetic arguments, as other major reversals of the positions of other racial groups or subgroups would undermine the later genetic determinism of other intellectuals.

This is not to say that there were no great differences in achievements among different races, either within societies or between societies, as of a given time, nor that all such differences reversed over time, though many did. But once the automatic link between genetics and achievement is broken, it ceases to be a weighty presumption, even in the case of groups that have never been leaders in achievement. Whatever non-genetic factors have been able to produce profound differences in other situations cannot be ruled out *a priori* for any group, and therefore it remains a question to be examined empirically in each particular case— that is, if science is to be something more than an incantation invoked to buttress an ideology and silence its critics.

Much empirical evidence of large and consequential differences among racial or ethnic groups, as well as social classes, accumulated in the late nineteenth and early twentieth centuries. Studies of the histories of families, as well as the spread of mental testing, and sociological studies of differences in crime rates and educational achievements among children from different backgrounds, even when attending the same schools, added weight to the case made by those promoting genetic determinism. Contrary to later verbal fashions, these were not simply "perceptions" or "stereotypes." These were painstakingly established facts, despite the serious problems with the inferences drawn from those facts— such as Madison Grant's sweeping pronouncement, "race is everything."[4]

THE PROGRESSIVE ERA

The Progressive era in early twentieth century America was perhaps the high-water mark of "scientific" theories of racial differences. The increasing immigration from Europe, and especially the shift in its origins from Northern and Western Europe to Eastern and Southern Europe, raised questions about the racial quality of the new people flooding into the country. The beginning of the mass migrations of American blacks from the South to the Northern cities, and their concentration in ghettos there, raised similar questions during the same era. Empirical data on group differences in crime rates, disease rates, mental test scores, and school performances fed all these concerns.

Two huge compilations of empirical data in early twentieth century America stand out particularly. One was the huge, multi-volume report of the federal immigration commission headed by Senator William P. Dillingham and published in 1911. This report showed, among other things, that with children who attended elementary school three-quarters of the school days or more, 30 percent of native-born white children had been denied promotion to the next grade, compared to 61 percent of native-born black children and 67 percent of the children of immigrant Polish Jews.[5] The other huge source of data about differences among racial or ethnic groups during this period was the mental testing of more than 100,000 soldiers by the U.S. Army during the First World War.[6] The proportions of soldiers with different ancestries who exceeded the American national norms on mental tests were as follows:[7]

English	67 percent
German	49 percent
Irish	26 percent
Russian	19 percent
Italian	14 percent
Polish	12 percent

Men from Italy, Poland and Russia scored consistently at or near the bottom among immigrants from Europe on various mental tests, with American blacks scoring at the bottom among soldiers as a whole, though scoring only marginally lower than these Southern and Eastern European immigrants on these tests.[8] Among the civilian population, the same groups scored at or near the bottom in mental test scores, though in a slightly different order. Black children attending schools in Youngstown, Ohio, scored marginally higher on IQ tests than the children of Polish, Greek and other immigrants there.[9] In Massachusetts, a larger proportion of black school children scored over 120 on the IQ tests than did their schoolmates who were children of Polish, Italian or Portuguese immigrants.[10] During this era, Northern blacks had somewhat higher IQs than Southern blacks.[11]

Another curious fact, which received much less attention at the time, was that the Army tests in the First World War showed white soldiers from Georgia, Arkansas, Kentucky, and Mississippi scoring lower on mental tests than black soldiers from Ohio, Illinois, New York, and Pennsylvania.[12] However, the black population as a whole was overwhelmingly concentrated in the South at that time, which may explain why the Army tests showed blacks scoring below the immigrants that they scored above in civilian tests conducted where they both went to the same schools in the North.

Again, none of this was simply a matter of "perceptions," "stereotypes," or "prejudices." Differences among racial, ethnic and regional groups were very real, sometimes very large and very consequential. What was at issue were the *reasons* for those differences. Moreover, the reasons for such differences that were acceptable to intellectuals changed radically over the generations, much as their support for the First World War and their later pacifism marked drastic changes on that subject.

During the early twentieth century, demonstrable differences among groups were largely attributed to heredity and, during the late twentieth century, these differences were largely— if not solely— attributed to environment, including an environment of discrimination. Nevertheless, the same *general* vision of society prevailed among those who called themselves Progressives at the beginning of the twentieth century and those who called themselves liberals later in that century, however disparate their views on race were between these two eras. Theirs was the vision of the anointed as surrogate decision-makers in both periods, along with such corollaries as an expanded role for government and an expanded role for judges to re-interpret the Constitution, so as to loosen its restrictions on the powers of government.

Progressive-era intellectuals took a largely negative view of the new immigrants from Southern and Eastern Europe, as well as of American blacks in general. Because such a high proportion of the immigrants from Poland and Russia were Jews during this era, Carl Brigham— a leading authority on mental tests, and creator of the College Board's Scholastic Aptitude Test— asserted that the Army test results tended to "disprove the popular belief that the Jew is highly intelligent."[13] H.H. Goddard, who had administered mental tests to immigrant children on Ellis Island, declared: "These people cannot deal with abstractions."[14] Another giant of the mental-testing profession, L.M. Terman, author of the Stanford-Binet IQ test and creator of a decades-long study of people with IQs of 140 and above, likewise concluded from his study of racial minorities in the Southwest that children from such groups "cannot master abstractions."[15] It was widely accepted as more or less a matter of course during this era that blacks were incapable of mental performances comparable to whites, and the Army mental test results were taken as confirmation.

The Progressive era was also the heyday of eugenics, the attempt to prevent excessive breeding of the "wrong" kind of people— including, though not limited to, particular races. Eugenicists feared that people of lower mental capacity would reproduce on a larger scale than others, and thus over time bring about a decline in the average IQ in the nation.[16] *The New Republic* lamented "the multiplication of the unfit, the production of a horde of unwanted souls."[17]

In Britain, as in the United States, leaders and supporters of the eugenics movement included people on the left, such as John Maynard Keynes, who helped create the Cambridge Eugenics Society, as well as H.G. Wells, George Bernard Shaw, Harold Laski, Sidney Webb and Julian Huxley. Sidney Webb said, "as a nation we are breeding largely from our inferior stocks."[18] But eugenics was by no means exclusively a movement on the left, nor one without opponents on the left. Supporters of eugenics also included conservatives, among them both Neville Chamberlain and Winston Churchill.[19]

In America, among those to whom pioneer birth-control advocate Margaret Sanger took her message was the Ku Klux Klan. Madison Grant's book *The Passing of the Great Race*, expressing fears of a loss of hegemony by whites in general and Nordics in particular, was a landmark book of its era. It was not only a best seller in the United States, it was translated into French, Norwegian and— most fatefully— German. Hitler called it his "Bible."[20]

Despite its international influence, *The Passing of the Great Race* offered extremely little evidence for its sweeping conclusions. The great bulk of the book was a historical account of Alpine, Mediterranean and Nordic peoples in Europe and of the Aryan languages. Yet most of Madison Grant's sweeping conclusions and the policies he recommended were about America— about the "inferior races among our immigrants,"[21] about the need for eugenics[22] and for "laws against miscegenation."[23] He asserted that "Negroes have demonstrated throughout recorded time that they are a stationary species and that they do not possess the potentiality of progress or initiative from within."[24] Yet, as Grant himself said, "the three main European races are the subject of this book,"[25] which contained virtually no factual information about blacks, but only opaque pronouncements. Even Grant's rankings of European groups are essentially pronouncements, with little or no empirical evidence or analysis, despite an abundance of miscellaneous and often arcane information.

What *The Passing of the Great Race* did have was a great display of erudition, or apparent erudition, using numerous technical terms unfamiliar to most people— "brachycephalic skulls,"[26] "Armenoids,"[27] "Paleolithic man,"[28] the "Massagetæ,"[29] "Zendavesta,"[30] the "Aryan Tokharian language,"[31] and the "Miocene" and "Pliocene" eras,[32] as well as such statements as "The Upper Paleolithic embraces all the postglacial stages down to the Neolithic and includes the subdivisions of the Aurignacian, Solutrean, Magdalenian and Azilian."[33] But this all served as an impressive backdrop for unrelated conclusions.

Among Madison Grant's conclusions were that "race lies at the base of all the manifestation of modern society."[34] He also deplored "a sentimental belief in the sanctity of human life," when that is used "to prevent both the elimination of defective infants and the sterilization of such adults as are themselves of no value to the community."[35] He feared "the resurgence of the lower races at the expense of the Nordics"[36] and the "prevailing lack of true race consciousness" among the latter.[37] He saw the immigrants arriving in America as the "sweepings" of the "jails and asylums" of Europe.[38] More generally, he said:

> There exists to-day a widespread and fatuous belief in the power of environment, as well as of education and opportunity to alter heredity, which arises from the dogma of the brotherhood of man, derived in its turn from the loose thinkers of the French Revolution and their American mimics.[39]

> The man of the old stock is being crowded out of many country districts by these foreigners just as he is to-day being literally driven off the streets of New York City by the swarms of Polish Jews.[40]

> We Americans must realize that the altruistic ideals which have controlled our social development during the past century and the maudlin sentimentalism that has made America "an asylum for the oppressed," are sweeping the nation toward a racial abyss.[41]

That *The Passing of the Great Race* was taken seriously says much about the times. But Madison Grant was by no means a fringe crank or an ignorant redneck. He was born into a wealthy family in New York City and was educated at Yale and the Columbia University law school. He was a member of numerous exclusive social clubs. Politically, he was a Progressive and an activist on issues important to Progressives, such as conservation, endangered species, municipal reform and the creation of national parks, as well as being a driving force behind the creation of the world's largest zoo in the Bronx.[42] *The Passing of the Great Race* was recommended not only in a popular publication like *The Saturday Evening Post* but was also reviewed in *Science*, published by the American Association for the Advancement of Science.[43] The maps for a later book of his were prepared with the help of the American Geographical Society.[44]

Madison Grant's thesis elaborated themes introduced by others before him, such as Progressive sociologist Edward A. Ross, who coined the term "race suicide" to describe the demographic replacement of the existing American stock over time by immigrants with higher birthrates from Southern and Eastern Europe, those whom prominent economist Francis A. Walker had even earlier described as "beaten men from beaten races."[45]

Professor Ross declared that "no one can doubt that races differ in intellectual ability"[46] and lamented an "unanticipated result" of widespread access to medical advances— namely "the brightening of the survival prospect of the ignorant, the stupid, the careless and the very poor in comparison with those of the intelligent, the bright, the responsible and the thrifty."[47] Ross' concerns were raised not only about people from different classes but also about the new and massive numbers of immigrants:

> Observe immigrants not as they come travel-wan up the gang-plank, nor as they issue toil-begrimed from pit's mouth or mill gate, but in their gatherings, washed, combed, and in their Sunday best. You are struck by the fact that from ten to twenty per cent. are hirsute, low-browed, big-faced persons of obviously low mentality. Not that they suggest evil. They simply look out of place in black clothes and stiff collar, since clearly they belong in skins, in wattled huts at the close of the Great Ice Age. These oxlike men are descendants of those *who always stayed behind*. . . To the practised eye, the physiognomy of certain groups unmistakably proclaims inferiority of type.[48]

According to Professor Ross, "the new immigrants are inferior in looks to the old immigrants,"[49] apparently because the new immigrants were from Eastern and Southern Europe, unlike earlier immigrants from Northern and Western Europe. As Ross put it:

> The fusing of American with German and Scandinavian immigrants was only a reblending of kindred stocks, for Angles, Jutes, Danes, and Normans were wrought of yore into the fiber of the English breed. But the human varieties being collected in this country by the naked action of economic forces are too dissimilar to blend without producing a good many faces of a "chaotic constitution."[50]

Nor were the differences between the old immigrants and the new limited to intellect or physical appearance, according to Ross: "That the Mediterranean peoples are morally below the races of northern Europe is as certain as any social fact."[51] Moreover, these differences were said to be due to people from Northern Europe surpassing people from Southern Europe "in innate ethical endowment."[52] Ross declared, "I see no reason why races may not differ as much in moral and intellectual traits as obviously they do in bodily traits."[53] Black Americans were mentioned in passing as "several millions of an inferior race."[54] To Ross, the survival of a superior race and culture depended on awareness of, and pride in, that superiority:

> The superiority of a race cannot be preserved without *pride of blood* and an uncompromising attitude toward the lower races. . . Since the higher culture should be kept pure as well as the higher blood, that race is stronger which, down to the cultivator or the artisan, has *a strong sense of its superiority.*[55]

Francis A. Walker was a leading economist of the second half of the nineteenth century. He was not a Progressive, by any means, but his views on immigrants from Southern and Eastern Europe were views that later became dominant in the Progressive era of the early twentieth century. He proposed strict restrictions on immigration, not only quantitatively, but qualitatively. He proposed to measure quality by requiring each immigrant to post a $100 bond upon entering the country— a sum vastly more than most Jewish, Italian or other immigrants from Eastern Europe or Southern Europe had with them at that time. He said that the restrictions he proposed "would not prevent tens of thousands of thrifty Swedes, Norwegians, Germans, and men of other nationalities coming hither at their own charges, since great numbers of these people now bring more than that amount of money with them."[56] Such a requirement, he said, would "raise the average quality, socially and industrially, of the immigrants actually entering the country."[57]

Walker saw a need to protect "the American standard of living, and the quality of American citizenship from degradation through the tumultuous access of vast throngs of ignorant and brutalized peasantry from the countries of eastern and southern Europe."[58] He pointed out that, in earlier times, immigrants "came almost exclusively from western or northern Europe" and "immigrants from southern Italy, Hungary, Austria, and Russia together made up hardly more than one per cent of our immigration." Now those proportions had changed completely, bringing "vast masses of peasantry, degraded below our utmost conceptions." He said: "They are beaten men from beaten races; representing the worst failures in the struggle for existence."[59]

Without restrictions on immigration, Professor Walker declared that "every foul and stagnant pool of population in Europe," from places where "no breath of intellectual life has stirred for ages," would be "decanted upon our shores."[60] Nor were the people of Eastern and Southern Europe the only ones dismissed as hopeless by Walker. The indigenous American Indians Walker dismissed as "savages," who were "without forethought and without self-control, singularly susceptible to evil influences, with strong animal appetites and no intellectual tastes or aspirations to hold those appetites in check."[61]

Another prominent contemporary economist, Richard T. Ely, one of the founders of the American Economic Association, was similarly dismissive of blacks, saying that they "are for the most part grown-up children, and should be treated as such."[62] Professor Ely was also concerned about classes that he considered inferior: "We must give to the most hopeless classes left behind in our social progress custodial care with the highest possible development and with segregation of sexes and confinement to prevent reproduction."[63]

Richard T. Ely was not only a Progressive during the Progressive era, he espoused the kinds of ideas that defined the Progressive era, years before that era began. He rejected free market economics[64] and saw government power as something to be applied "to the amelioration of the conditions under which people live or work." Far from seeing government intervention as a reduction of freedom, he redefined freedom, so that the "regulation by the power of the state of these industrial and other social relations existing among men is a condition of freedom." While state action might "lessen the amount of theoretical liberty" it would "increase control over nature in the individual, and promote the growth of practical liberty."[65]

Like other Progressives, Richard T. Ely advocated the cause of conservation, of labor unions, and favored the "coercive philanthropy" of the state.[66] He said, "I believe that such natural resources as forests and mineral wealth should belong to the people" and also believed that "highways or railroads as well as telegraph and parcels post" should also be owned by "the community." He also favored "public ownership" of municipal utilities[67] and declared that "labor unions should be legally encouraged in their efforts for shorter hours and higher wages" and that "inheritance and income taxes should be generally extended."[68] In short, in the course of his long lifetime Professor Ely was a Progressive before, during and after the Progressive era.

Rejecting the economic analysis of free market wage rates by such leading economists of that era as Alfred Marshall in England and John Bates Clark in the United States, economists of a Progressive orientation advocated minimum wage laws, as a way of preventing "low-wage races" such as Chinese immigrants from lowering the standard of living of American workers. Professor John R. Commons, for example, said "The competition has no respect for the superior races," so that "the race with lowest necessities displaces others." Professor Arthur Holcombe of Harvard, and a president of the American Political Science Association, referred approvingly of Australia's minimum wage law as a means to "protect the white Australian's standard of living from the invidious competition of the colored races, particularly of the Chinese."[69]

Eugenics, however, was not confined to trying to reduce the reproduction of particular races. Many of its advocates targeted also people of the sort whom Harvard economist Frank Taussig called "those saturated with alcohol or tainted with hereditary disease," as well as "the irretrievable criminals and tramps." If it was not feasible to "chloroform them once and for all," Professor Taussig said, then "at least they can be segregated, shut up in refuges and asylums, and prevented from propagating their kind."[70] In Sweden in later years, Nobel Prizewinning economist Gunnar Myrdal supported programs which sterilized 60,000 people from 1941 through 1975.[71]

Many academics, including some of great distinction, were supporters of eugenics during the Progressive era. Professor Irving Fisher of Yale, the leading American monetary economist of his day, was one of the founders of the American Eugenics Society. Professor Fisher advocated the prevention of the "breeding of the worst" by "isolation in public institutions and in some cases by surgical operation."[72] Professor Henry Rogers Seager of Columbia University, who would become sufficiently recognized to be selected as president of the American Economic Association, likewise said that "we must courageously cut off lines of heredity that have been proved to be undesirable," even if that requires "isolation or sterilization."[73] Stanford University's president David Starr Jordan declared that a nation's "blood" was what "determines its history."[74] Eugenics outlasted the Progressive era. As late as 1928, there were 376 college courses devoted to eugenics.[75]

Those who promoted genetic determinism and eugenics were neither uneducated nor fringe cranks. Quite the contrary. Edward A. Ross, Francis A. Walker and Richard T. Ely all had Ph.D.s from leading universities and were professors at leading universities. Edward A. Ross was the author of 28 books, whose sales were estimated at approximately half a million copies, and he was regarded as one of the founders of the profession of sociology in the United States.[76] He held a Ph.D. in economics from Johns Hopkins University and, at various times, served as Secretary of the American Economic Association as well as President of the American Sociological Association, and head of the American Civil Liberties Union. Among the places where his articles appeared were the *Annals of the American Academy of Political and Social Science.*

Ross was in the mainstream of Progressive intellectuals at the highest levels. He was a man of the left who had supported Eugene V. Debs in the 1894 Pullman strike and had advocated public ownership and regulation of public utilities. Active as a public intellectual in print and on the lecture circuit, Professor Ross referred to "us liberals" as people who speak up "for public interests against powerful selfish private interests," and denounced those who disagreed with his views as unworthy "kept" spokesmen for special interests, a "mercenary corps" as contrasted with "us champions of the social welfare."[77]

Roscoe Pound credited Ross with setting him "in the path the world is moving in."[78] Ross praised the muckrakers of his day and was also said to have been influential with Progressive Presidents Theodore Roosevelt and Woodrow Wilson.[79] The introduction to one of Ross' books included a letter of fulsome praise from TR.[80] The voters' repudiation of the Progressives in the years after the Woodrow Wilson presidency Ross referred to as the "Great Ice Age (1919–31)."[81] In self-righteousness, as well as in ideology, he was a Progressive, a man of the left.

Francis A. Walker was similarly prominent in the economics profession of his day. He was the first president of the American Economic Association— and the Francis A. Walker medal, created in 1947, was the highest award given by the American Economic Association until 1977, when it was discontinued as a result of the creation of a Nobel Prize in economics. Professor Walker was also General Walker in the Union army during the Civil War. He was, at various times, also president of the American Statistical Association and the Massachusetts Institute of Technology. He was also in charge of the ninth and tenth censuses of the United States, a Commissioner of Indian Affairs, and was elected a fellow of the American Academy of Arts and Sciences.

After Walker's death in 1897, commemorative articles appeared in the scholarly journal of the American Statistical Association, in the *Quarterly Journal of Economics*, the first scholarly journal of the economics profession in the United States, published at Harvard, as well as in the *Journal of Political Economy*, published at the University of Chicago, and an obituary also appeared in the *Economic Journal*, England's premier scholarly journal of the economics profession.

Richard T. Ely received his Ph.D. *summa cum laude* from the University of Heidelberg and was the author of many books, one of which sold more than a million copies.[82] Among the prominent people who were his students were the already mentioned Edward A. Ross and Woodrow Wilson, both of whom studied under him at Johns Hopkins University.[83] He was also considered "a major contributing force in making the University of Wisconsin a vital institution wielding a profound influence upon the political economy of the State and the nation."[84] Ely has been called "the father of institutional economics,"[85] the field in which one of his students, John R. Commons, made his name at the University of Wisconsin. Richard T. Ely's death in 1943 was marked by tributes on both sides of the Atlantic, including an obituary in Britain's *Economic Journal*.[86] On into the twenty-first century, one of the honors awarded annually by the American Economic Association to a distinguished economist has been an invitation to give the association's Richard T. Ely Lecture.

In short, Edward A. Ross, Francis A. Walker and Richard T. Ely were not only "in the mainstream"— to use a term that has become common in our times— they were among the elite of the mainstream. But that was no more indication of the validity of what they said then than it is among today's elite of the mainstream.

While Madison Grant was not an academic scholar, he moved among prominent members of the intelligentsia. His closest friends included George Bird Grinnell, editor of the elite sportsman's magazine *Forest and Stream*, and Henry Fairfield Osborn, a world-renowned paleontologist who coined the term "tyrannosaurus rex." Osborn said, in the wake of mass mental testing: "We have learned once and for all that the negro is not like us."[87] In short, Madison Grant, Edward A. Ross, Francis A. Walker and Richard T. Ely were part of the intellectual currents of the times, in an era when leading intellectuals saw mental test results as confirming innate racial differences, when immigration was severely restricted for racial reasons, and when the Ku Klux Klan was revived and spread beyond the South, becoming an especially strong political force in the Midwest. As even a critical biographer of Madison Grant said:

> Grant was not an evil man. He did not wake up in the morning and think to himself: "Hmm, I wonder what vile deeds I can commit today." To the contrary, he was by all accounts a sweet, considerate, erudite, and infinitely charming figure.[88]

Madison Grant also moved in socially elite and politically Progressive circles. Theodore Roosevelt welcomed Grant's entry into an exclusive social club that TR had founded.[89] Later, Grant became friends for a time with Franklin D. Roosevelt, addressing him in letters as "My dear Frank," while FDR reciprocated by addressing him as "My dear Madison."[90] The two men met while serving on a commission as civic-minded citizens, and the fact that both suffered crippling illnesses during the 1920s created a personal bond. But Madison Grant's ideas moved far beyond such genteel circles in America. They were avidly seized upon in Nazi Germany, though Grant's death in 1937 spared him from learning of the ultimate consequences of such ideas, which culminated in the Holocaust.

George Horace Lorimer, long-time editor of the *Saturday Evening Post*, was another major supporter of the Progressive movement in the early twentieth century and his magazine, with a readership of four to five million readers per week,[91] carried weight politically and socially. He supported both Theodore Roosevelt and Progressive Senator Albert Beveridge.[92] In proposing immigration restrictions, Lorimer— like many others of that era— invoked "science" as opposed to "the Pollyanna school."[93] In an editorial in the *Saturday Evening Post*, Lorimer warned against "our racial degeneration" as a result of immigration, which he said could end with Americans having to "forfeit our high estate and join the lowly ranks of the mongrel races."[94]

In the early 1920s, Lorimer assigned novelist and future Pulitzer Prize winner Kenneth L. Roberts to write a series of articles on immigration for the *Saturday Evening Post*. In one of these articles Roberts referred to "the better-class Northern and Western Europeans" who "are particularly fine types of immigrants," as contrasted with "the queer, alien, mongrelized people of Southeastern Europe."[95] These articles were later republished as a book titled *Why Europe Leaves Home*. In this book, Roberts said, among other things, "the Jews of Poland are human parasites,"[96] that people from the Austro-Hungarian Empire were "inconceivably backward."[97] He added:

> The American nation was founded and developed by the Nordic race, but if a few more million members of the Alpine, Mediterranean and Semitic races are poured among us, the result must inevitably be a hybrid race of people as worthless and futile as the good-for-nothing mongrels of Central America and Southeastern Europe.[98]

Like many others of that era, Roberts invoked the notion of a "scientific" approach to immigration law,[99] while contrasting "the desirable immigrants from Northwestern Europe" with the "undesirables" who "came from Southern and Eastern European countries."[100]

Progressive muckraking journalist George Creel, a former member of Woodrow Wilson's administration, wrote articles on immigration in 1921 and 1922 in *Collier's* magazine, another leading mass circulation publication of that era. In these articles he made the familiar contrast between the peoples of Northern and Western Europe with the people of Eastern and Southern Europe, using the familiar nomenclature of that time, which called the former Nordics and the latter Alpine and Mediterranean peoples:

> The men and women who first came to America were Nordic— clean-blooded, strong-limbed people from England, Ireland, Scotland, Scandinavia, Belgium, Holland, Germany, and France. The millions that followed them, for a full two centuries, were also Nordic, holding the same customs, ideas, and ideals, fitting into the life they found as skin fits the hand.
>
> Not until 1880 was there any vital change in the character of immigration, and then commenced the tidal waves of two new stocks— the Alpine from central Europe, Slavs for the most part, and the Mediterranean, the small swarthy peoples from southern Italy, Greece, Spain, and northern Africa.[101]

These latter immigrants, Creel described as the "failures, unfits, and misfits of the Old World."[102] Creel said, "those coming from eastern Europe were morally, physically, and mentally the worst in the history of immigration."[103]

While H.L. Mencken was another prominent intellectual during the Progressive era, he was by no means a Progressive. Yet his view of blacks was very much like that of other intellectuals of the times. Writing in 1908, he wrote of "the hopelessly futile and fatuous effort to improve the negroes of the Southern United States by education." He added:

> It is apparent, on brief reflection, that the negro, no matter how much he is educated, must remain, as a race, in a condition of subservience; that he must remain the inferior of the stronger and more intelligent white man so long as he retains racial differentiation. Therefore, the effort to educate him has awakened in his mind ambitions and aspirations which, in the very nature of things, must go unrealized, and so, while gaining nothing whatever materially, he has lost all his old contentment, peace of mind and happiness. Indeed, it is a commonplace of observation in the United States that the educated and refined negro is invariably a hopeless, melancholy, embittered and despairing man.[104]

Similar views of blacks were expressed in other early writings by H.L. Mencken, though blacks were not the only group viewed negatively in those writings:

> The negro loafer is not a victim of restricted opportunity and oppression. There are schools for him, and there is work for him, and he disdains both. That his forty-odd years of freedom have given him too little opportunity to show his mettle is a mere theory of the chair. As a matter of fact, the negro, in the mass, seems to be going backward. The most complimentary thing that can be said of an individual of the race today is that he is as industrious and honest a man as his grandfather, who was a slave. There are exceptional negroes of intelligence and ability, I am well aware, just as there are miraculous Russian Jews who do not live in filth; but the great bulk of the race is made up of inefficients.[105]

However, by 1926, H.L. Mencken had changed his position somewhat. In a review of a book of essays by leading black intellectuals, edited by Alain Locke, himself a leading black intellectual of the times, Mencken wrote:

> This book, it seems to me, is a phenomenon of immense significance. What it represents is the American Negro's final emancipation from his inferiority complex, his bold decision to go it alone. That inferiority complex, until very recently, conditioned all of his thinking, even (and perhaps especially) when he was bellowing most vociferously for his God-given rights.
> . . .
> As I have said, go read the book. And, having read it, ask yourself the simple question: could you imagine a posse of *white* Southerners doing anything so dignified, so dispassionate, so striking? . . . As one who knows the South better than most, and has had contact with most of its intellectuals, real and Confederate, I must say frankly that I can imagine no such thing. Here, indeed, the Negro challenges the white Southerner on a common ground, and beats him hands down.[106]

Yet Mencken was by no means sanguine about the prospects of the black population as a whole:

> The vast majority of the people of their race are but two or three inches removed from gorillas: it will be a sheer impossibility, for a long, long while, to interest them in anything above pork-chops and bootleg gin.[107]

Like many other intellectuals of the early twentieth century, H.L. Mencken in 1937 favored eugenics measures— in this case, voluntary sterilization of males, encouraged by rewards to be supplied by private philanthropy. As in the past, he included white Southerners among those considered undesirable. He suggested that the answers to many social problems would be "to sterilize large numbers of American freemen, both white and black, to the end that they could no longer beget their kind." For this "the readiest way to induce them to submit would be to indemnify them in cash." The alternative, he said, would be "supporting an ever-increasing herd of morons for all eternity."[108]

Not all eugenicists were racial determinists, as Mencken's inclusion of white Southerners in his eugenics agenda in 1937 indicated. In England, H.G. Wells rejected the singling out of particular races for extinction, though he recommended that undesirable people of whatever race be targeted.[109] Writing in 1916, Wells said:

> Now I am a writer rather prejudiced against the idea of nationality; my habit of thought is cosmopolitan; I hate and despise a shrewish suspicion of foreigners and foreign ways ; a man who can look me in the face, laugh with me, speak truth and deal fairly, is my brother, though his skin is as black as ink or as yellow as an evening primrose.[110]

American novelist and radical Jack London, however, declared, "the Anglo-Saxon is a race of mastery" and is "best fitted for survival." He said, "the inferior races must undergo destruction, or some humane form of economic slavery, is inevitable."[111] While Jack London was a man of the left during the Progressive era, he was not a Progressive. He boldly declared himself a socialist.

Woodrow Wilson, one of two American presidents who was also an intellectual in our sense of one who for years earned his living from the production of ideas (the other being Theodore Roosevelt), praised the movie *The Birth of A Nation*, which glorified the Ku Klux Klan, and had a private showing of it in the White House, to which prominent political figures were invited.[112] It was during the Progressive administration of Woodrow Wilson that the Bureau of the Census and the Bureau of Printing and Engraving began to segregate black and white employees. The Post Office Department not only began to segregate its black and white employees in Washington during the Wilson administration, but also began to fire and downgrade black postal employees in the South, as did the Department of the Treasury. President Wilson expressed his approval of these actions.[113]

The academic world was by no means exempt from the racial and social beliefs of the times. In early twentieth century America, during an era when most applicants to even highly prestigious colleges were admitted, there were both formal and informal restrictions on the admissions of Jews, Harvard being one of the few institutions to openly admit imposing quota limits, though a 1909 article characterized anti-Semitism as "more dominant at Princeton" (under Woodrow Wilson) than at any of the other institutions surveyed. In 1910, students at Williams College demonstrated against the admission of Jews. In 1922, Yale's dean of admission said: "The opinion is general in the Faculty that the proportion of those in college whose racial elements are such as not to permit of assimilation has been exceeded and that the most noticeable representatives among those regarded as undesirable are the Jewish boys."[114]

Such views on race or ethnicity were not inevitably entailed by the principles of Progressivism, though they were not precluded by those principles either. During the Progressive era itself, Theodore Roosevelt had a very different view of the *potential* of blacks than did many other Progressives. In response to a British historian who expressed a fear that the black and yellow races would rise in the world to the point of challenging the white race, Theodore Roosevelt said: "By that time the descendant of the negro may be as intellectual as the Athenian."[115] Moreover, he also believed in equal opportunity for other minorities.[116]

Nevertheless, Roosevelt's low estimate of the *contemporary* level of knowledge and understanding among black Americans[117] might place him under at least a suspicion of racism by those today who project contemporary standards back into the past, or who perhaps think of the black population of the past as if they were simply today's black population living in an earlier time, rather than a population which in that era included millions of people who had not yet acquired even the ability to read and write.

One of the ironies of Madison Grant's theories was that he was a descendant of Scots who emigrated after the failed uprisings against the English in 1745. In earlier centuries, Scotland had been one of the most backward nations on the fringes of European civilization, even though Grant classified the Scots as Nordics, who were supposedly superior intellectually. Later, Scots had a spectacular rise to the forefront of European and world civilization, in too brief a time— as history is measured— for there to have been any major change in the genetic make-up of Scotland's population. In short, the history of his own ancestral homeland provided some of the strongest evidence against Grant's theories of genetic determinism. So do other major reversals in technological and other leadership among nations, races and civilizations, such as the reversal of the positions of China and Europe already noted. There are many peoples and nations that have experienced their "golden age," only to later fall behind, or even be conquered by, their erstwhile inferiors.

The wider the sweep of history that is surveyed, the more dramatic reversals of the relative positions of nations and races there are. A tenth-century Muslim scholar noted that Europeans grow more pale the farther north you go and also that the "farther they are to the north the more stupid, gross, and brutish they are."[118] However offensive this correlation between skin color and intellectual development may seem today, there is no reason in history to challenge it as an empirical generalization, as of that particular time. Mediterranean Europe was more advanced than northern Europe for centuries, beginning in ancient times, when the Greeks and Romans laid many of the foundations of Western civilization, at a time when the peoples of Britain and Scandinavia lived in illiterate and far less advanced societies.

Like the tenth-century Muslim scholar, Madison Grant saw a correlation between skin color and intelligence, but he explicitly attributed that correlation to genetics. Among other things, he explained the over-representation of mulattoes among the black elite of his day by their Caucasian genes, and Edward Byron Reuter made an empirical sociological study of the same phenomenon, reaching the same conclusion.[119] In a later period, intellectuals would explain the same phenomenon by the bias of whites in favor of people who looked more like themselves.

Regardless of what either theory says, the facts show that the actual skills and behavior of blacks and mulattoes had historically been demonstrably different, especially in nineteenth and early twentieth century America.

These were not mere "perceptions" or "stereotypes," as so many inconvenient observations have been labeled. A study of nineteenth century Philadelphia, for example, found crime rates higher among the black population than among the mulatto population.[120] It is not necessary to believe that crime rates are genetically determined, but it is also not necessary to believe that it was all just a matter of perceptions by whites.[121]

During the era of slavery, mulattoes were often treated differently from blacks, especially when the mulattoes were the offspring of the slave owner. This difference in treatment existed not only in the United States but throughout the Western Hemisphere. Mulattoes were a much higher proportion of the population of "free persons of color" than they were of the populations of slaves throughout the Western Hemisphere, and women were far more often freed than were men.[122] These initial differences, based on personal favoritism, led to long-term differences based on earlier opportunities to begin acquiring human capital as free people, generations before the Emancipation Proclamation.

In short, "free persons of color" had a generations-long head start in acculturation, urbanization and general experience as free people. The rate of literacy reached by the "free persons of color" in 1850 would not be reached by the black population as a whole until 70 years later.[123] It was 1920 before the black population of the United States as a whole became as urbanized as the "free persons of color" were in 1860.[124] Neither within groups nor between groups can differences be discussed in the abstract, in a world where the concrete is what determines people's fates. Among Americans of African descent, as within and between other groups, *people are not random events* to which statistical probability theories can be blithely applied— and correlation is not causation.

Against the background of head starts by those freed from slavery generations ahead of others, it is not so surprising that, in the middle of the twentieth century, most of the Negro professionals in Washington, D.C. were by all indications descendants of the antebellum "free persons of color"[125]— a group that was never more than 14 percent of the American Negro population.[126] Because many of these professionals— such as doctors, lawyers and teachers— worked primarily or exclusively within the black community in mid-twentieth-century Washington, favoritism by *contemporary* whites had little or nothing to do with their success, even though the human capital which produced that success developed ultimately from the favoritism shown their ancestors a century or more earlier.

Neither genetics nor contemporary environment is necessary to explain differences in human capital between blacks and mulattoes— differences that were much more pronounced in earlier years than today, after the black population as a whole has had more time and opportunities as free people to acquire more human capital. Similarly, neither genetics nor contemporary environment is necessary to explain differences in skills, behavior, attitudes and values among other racial groups or sub-groups in many other countries around the world, since many of these groups differed greatly in their history, in their geographic settings and in other ways.

Madison Grant asserted that "the intelligence and ability of a colored person are in pretty direct proportion to the amount of white blood he has, and that most of the positions of leadership, influence, and prominence in the Negro race are held not by real Negroes but by Mulattoes, many of whom have very little Negro blood. This is so true that to find a black Negro in a conspicuous position is a matter of comment."[127] But, like so much else that was said by him and by others of like mind, it verbally eternalized a contemporary pattern by attributing that pattern to genetics, just as many Progressive-era intellectuals disdained the peoples of Southern Europe, who had by all indices once been far more advanced in ancient times than the Nordics who were said to be genetically superior. The Greeks and Romans had the Parthenon and the Coliseum, not to mention literature and giants of philosophy, at a time when there was not a single building in Britain, a country inhabited at that time by illiterate tribes.

Chapter 4

Internal Responses to Disparities

Although economic and social inequalities among racial and ethnic groups have attracted much attention from intellectuals, seldom today has this attention been directed primarily toward how the less economically successful and less socially prestigious groups might improve themselves by availing themselves of the culture of others around them, so as to become more productive and compete more effectively with other groups in the economy. When David Hume urged his fellow eighteenth-century Scots to master the English language,[1] as they did, both he and they were following a pattern very different from the pattern of most minority intellectuals and their respective groups in other countries around the world. The spectacular rise of the Scots in the eighteenth and nineteenth centuries— eventually surpassing the English in engineering and medicine,[2] for example— was also an exception, rather than the rule.

A much more common pattern has been one in which the intelligentsia have demanded an equality of economic outcomes and of social recognition, irrespective of the skills, behavior or performance of the group to which they belong or on whose behalf they spoke. In some countries today, any claim that intergroup differences in outcomes are results of intergroup differences in skills, behavior or performance are dismissed by the intelligentsia as false "perceptions," "prejudices," or "stereotypes," or else are condemned as "blaming the victim." Seldom are any of these assertions backed up by empirical evidence or logical analysis that would make them anything more than arbitrary assertions that happen to be in vogue among contemporary intellectual elites.

In direct contrast with the Scots, who mastered the language of the English— and the broader range of knowledge, skills and culture to which that language gave them access— other groups in a position to rise by acquiring the knowledge and skills available in another language or culture have resented having to advance in that way.

In the days of the Russian Empire, for example, most of the merchants, artisans, and industrialists in the Baltic port city of Riga were German,[3] even though Germans were less than one-fourth of that city's population.[4] Education at Dorpat University in Riga was conducted in German, as was most of the educational activity in the city.[5] Not only in Riga, but in Latvia as a whole, the upper classes were mostly German and the lower classes mostly Latvian. However, those Latvians who wanted to rise could become part of the elite German culture and intermarry into the German community. But a newly emerging Latvian educated class, many educated at Dorpat University, resented having to become culturally German in order to rise, and initiated the politics of ethnic identity instead.[6] They saw Latvians as a people "consigned by long oppression to lowly stations in life."[7]

A very similar process occurred in the Habsburg Empire, where the Germans in Bohemia were an educated elite and where Czechs there who wanted to rise into that elite could do so by acquiring the German language and culture. But a new Czech intelligentsia, including university students and school teachers, promoted Czech cultural nationalism.[8] Czech nationalists, for example, insisted that street signs in Prague, which had been in both Czech and German, henceforth be exclusively in Czech.[9] In the town of Budweis, Czech nationalists demanded that a quota of Czech music be played by the town orchestra.[10] Symbolism— including intolerance toward other people's symbols— has often marked the efforts of an ethnic intelligentsia.

The rising indigenous intelligentsia— whether in Latvia, Bohemia or elsewhere— tended to treat the cultural advantages of Germans as a *social* injustice, against which they mobilized other members of their ethnic group to oppose Germans and German culture. Whether in the Baltic or in Bohemia, the Germans tended to be more cosmopolitan, and initially resisted efforts by the newly arising indigenous intelligentsia to fragment society along ethnic lines. But the persistent and increasing promotion of ethnic identity by the newly rising ethnic intelligentsia eventually led the Germans to abandon their cosmopolitanism and defend themselves as Germans.[11] The net result in both countries was ethnic polarization, often under the banner of some variation of "social justice," requiring the lagging group to be put on a par through some process other than their own acquisition of the same knowledge and skills as others.

Similar polarization has been produced in other countries with the rise of a newly educated intelligentsia— usually educated in "soft" fields, rather than in the sciences or in other subjects that would produce marketable skills with which to compete with members of other ethnic groups who already had such skills and experience. One historical study referred to the "well-educated but underemployed" Czech young men who promoted ethnic identity in the nineteenth century[12]— a description that would apply to many ethnic identity promoters in other parts of Europe and Asia, as well as in the United States, then and now. The "educated unemployed" became a common expression in the twentieth century,[13] whether in Europe, Asia or elsewhere— and such people became common sources of ethnic polarization.

An international study of ethnic conflicts pointed out: "The very elites who were thought to be leading their peoples away from ethnic affiliations were commonly found to be in the forefront of ethnic conflict."[14] Romania between the two World Wars was a typical example:

> The years under review recorded a more visible presence of "the intellectual proletariat": schoolmasters, lawyers, students and university graduates. This social category continued to grow, but it met with great difficulties in asserting itself and gaining a satisfactory social status. Its members were handicapped by their precarious social situation and financial difficulties during their years of study. Most of them were "first-generation" intellectuals or the sons of teachers, priests or petty functionaries. They were the main source of the right-wing movements' audience and accounted for a high proportion of the antisemitic organizations' membership. As in Poland and Hungary, the relatively large numbers of Jews in the universities and free professions exacerbated the frustration of young people in their endeavors to carve out "a position" for themselves in the urban social structures.[15]

Among the leading promoters of anti-Semitism in Romania over the years have been an academic described as "the most important Romanian philosopher of the late nineteenth century,"[16] another academic described as "the greatest Romanian historian,"[17] and another intellectual described as "One of the most important twentieth-century Romanian national poets."[18]

Newly educated classes have been especially likely to specialize in softer subjects and to be prominent among those fostering hostility toward more advanced groups, while promoting ethnic "identity" movements, whether such movements have been mobilized against other ethnic groups, the existing authorities, or other targets. In various periods of history, the intelligentsia in general and newly educated people in particular have inflamed group against group, promoting discriminatory policies and/or physical violence in such disparate countries as India,[19] Hungary,[20] Nigeria,[21] Kazakhstan,[22] Romania,[23] Sri Lanka,[24] Canada,[25] and Czechoslovakia.[26]

Whether at the level of minority activists in a given society or at the level of leaders of national revolts against external imperial powers, promoters of nationalism have been disproportionately intellectuals— and intellectuals from a limited range of fields. "Few nationalist militants were engineers or economists, or professional administrators," as a study of nationalism said of the generation of African leaders during the transition from colonial status to that of independent nations in the twentieth century. For example, Kwame Nkrumah was a British-educated lawyer, Jomo Kenyatta an anthropologist, and Léopold Senghor a poet.[27] Much the same pattern could be found in other parts of the world as well. Leaders of the Basque separatist movement in Spain and of the Quebec separatist movement in Canada were also soft-subject intellectuals.[28]

In the less developed eastern regions of Europe, the rising intellectual class during the years between the two World Wars likewise tended to concentrate in the softer subjects, rather than in science or technology, and to seek careers in politics and government bureaucracies, rather than in industry or commerce. As a scholarly history of that era put it, institutions of higher education in East Central Europe turned out a "surplus academic proletariat" which could not be absorbed into "economically or socially functional employment" because they were trained primarily in law or the humanities.[29]

Romanian institutions of higher education were described as "numerically swollen, academically rather lax, and politically overheated," serving as "veritable incubators of surplus bureaucrats, politicians, and demagogues."[30]

Much the same pattern would be apparent decades later in Sri Lanka, which was all too typical of Asian Third World countries in having "a backlog of unemployed graduates" who had specialized in the humanities and the social sciences.[31] Ethnic leaders who would later promote the breakup of Yugoslavia, and the atrocities that followed in the last decade of the twentieth century, included professors in the humanities and the social sciences, as well as a novelist and a psychiatrist.[32] The mass slaughters in Kampuchea under the Khmer Rouge were likewise led principally by intellectuals, including teachers and academics.[33]

Historian A.J.P. Taylor has said that the first stage of nationalism "is led by university professors" and that "the second stage comes when the pupils of the professors get out into the world."[34] Whatever the actual sequence, the intelligentsia in many countries around the world have played a central role in promoting intergroup and international animosities and atrocities— and in trying to artificially preserve, revive, or fabricate past glories.

Conversely, the historic examples of dramatic self-improvement in nineteenth-century Japan and eighteenth-century Scotland— countries that set out to change themselves, rather than to blame others— concentrated on building tangible skills, such as in engineering and medicine in the case of Scotland, and science and technology in the case of Japan.* By contrast, in the twentieth century a whole generation of future Third World leaders who went to study in the West seldom concentrated on studying the science, technology or entrepreneurship that produced Western prosperity, but instead concentrated on the social theories and ideologies in vogue among Western intellectuals in academia and elsewhere. The countries they led after independence often paid a high price in economic stagnation or even retrogression, as well as in internal polarization that turned group against group.

---

* In addition to sending their young people abroad to study Western technology and science, the Japanese brought so many Scottish engineers to their own country that there was a Presbyterian church established in Japan.

Language politics has been one aspect of more general polarization that has poisoned relations between more prosperous and less prosperous groups in India, Malaysia, and Sri Lanka, among other places where the lagging majority tried to insulate themselves from competition with more successful minorities by making their own language a prerequisite for education and/or employment.[35] In Asia, as in Europe, Africa and the Western Hemisphere, the intelligentsia have been prominent among those pushing ethnic identity ideology and intergroup polarization.

Under such influences, Sri Lanka went from being a country whose record for harmonious relations between majority and minority was held up to the world as a model by many observers, in the mid-twentieth century, to a country whose later ethnic polarization produced decades of mob violence and then outright civil war, in which unspeakable atrocities were committed, on into the early twenty-first century.[36]

The polarization between Czechs and Germans in nineteenth century Bohemia took longer to reach the level of historic tragedy but nevertheless it did. A key turning point came when the new nation of Czechoslovakia was created in the twentieth century, from the breakup of the Habsburg Empire after the First World War, with the former kingdom of Bohemia now being Czechoslovakia's most economically and culturally advanced region— in part because of the Germans living in a section of that region called the Sudetenland. One indicator of the wide cultural differences among the various peoples of this small country was that the illiteracy rate in Bohemia was only 2 percent in 1921, while half the people in the province of Ruthenia were illiterate.[37] Much of Czechoslovakia's industry was located in Bohemia and a substantial proportion of it was in the hands of the Sudeten Germans.

Now armed with the power of government of their own country, Czech leaders set about "correcting" both historic and contemporary "injustices" — namely the fact that the Germans were more economically and otherwise advanced than the Czechs and other groups in the country. The government instituted preferential hiring of Czechs in the civil service and transferred capital from German and German-Jewish banks to Czech banks, as well as breaking up large German-owned estates into smaller farms, for the benefit of the Czech peasantry.[38] Violent German protests led to Czech soldiers shooting and killing more than fifty Germans,[39] setting the stage for a continuing bitter escalation of the polarization between Czechs and Germans, leading to larger tragedies in the decades that followed.

Nazi Germany annexed the Sudetenland in 1938 and then took over the rest of Czechoslovakia in 1939. With the country now under Nazi rule, the roles of Czechs and Germans were reversed, with brutal suppression of the Czechs that lasted until the defeat of Germany in 1945 allowed the Czechs to take control of the country once again. In the bitter backlash that followed, there was both official discrimination against Germans in Czechoslovakia and widespread unofficial and often lethal violence against Germans, more than three million of whom were expelled from the country, leaving behind a German population less than one-tenth of what it had once been.[40]

The Germans' skills and experience were of course expelled with them, and these were not easily replaced. Half a century later, there were still deserted towns and farmhouses in the Sudeten region, from which the Germans had been expelled[41]— mute testimony to the inconvenient fact that differences between Czechs and Germans were not simply matters of perceptions or injustices, unless one chooses to characterize historical circumstantial differences as injustices. All this was part of the price paid for seeking cosmic justice for intertemporal abstractions, in a world where maintaining peace and civility among flesh-and-blood contemporaries is often a major challenge by itself.

Whether in Europe, Asia, Africa or the Western Hemisphere, a common pattern among intellectuals has been to seek, or demand, equality of results without equality of causes— or on sheer presumptions of equality of causes. Nor have such demands been limited to intellectuals within the lagging groups, whether minorities or majorities. Outside intellectuals, including intellectuals in other countries, have often discussed statistical differences in incomes and other outcomes as "disparities," and "inequities" that need to be "corrected," as if they were discussing abstract people in an abstract world.

The corrections being urged are seldom corrections within the lagging groups, such as Hume urged upon his fellow Scots in the eighteenth century. Today, the prevailing tenets of multiculturalism declare all cultures equal, sealing members of lagging groups within a bubble of their current habits and practices, much as believers in multiculturalism have sealed themselves within a bubble of peer-consensus dogma.

There are certain possibilities that many among the intelligentsia cannot even acknowledge as possibilities, much less try to test empirically, which would be risking a whole vision of the world— and of themselves— on a roll of the dice. Chief among these is the possibility that the most fundamental disparity among people is in their disparities in wealth-generating capabilities, of which the disparities in income and wealth are results, rather than causes. Other disparities, whether in crime, violence and alcohol intake or other social pathology, may also have internal roots. But these possibilities as well are not allowed inside the sealed bubble of the prevailing vision.

One of the consequences of this vision is that blatant economic and other differences among groups, for which explanations due to factors internal to the lagging group are not allowed inside the sealed bubble of the multicultural vision, must be explained by external causes. If group *A* has higher incomes or higher other achievements than group *B*, then the vision of cosmic justice transforms *A*'s good fortune into *B*'s grievance— and not a grievance against fate, the gods, geography or the cosmos, but specifically a grievance against *A*. This formula has been applied around the world, whether turning Czechs against Germans, Malays against Chinese, Ugandans against Indians, Sinhalese against Tamils or innumerable other groups against those more successful than themselves.

The contribution of the intelligentsia to this process has often been to verbally conjure up a vision in which *A* has acquired wealth by taking it from *B*— the latter being referred to as "exploited," "dispossessed," or in some other verbal formulation that explains the economic disparity by a transfer of wealth from *B* to *A*. It does not matter if there is no speck of evidence that *B* was economically better off before *A* arrived on the scene. Nor does it matter how much evidence there may be that *B* became demonstrably worse off after *A* departed the scene, whether it was the Ugandan economy collapsing after the expulsions of Indians and Pakistanis in the 1970s, the desolation in the Sudeten region of Czechoslovakia after the Germans were expelled in 1945, or the continuing urban desolation of many black ghettoes across the United States, decades after the riots of the 1960s drove out many of the white-owned businesses that were supposedly exploiting ghetto residents.

Not only is empirical evidence that *A* made *B* poorer seldom considered necessary, considerable evidence that *A*'s presence kept *B* from being even poorer is often ignored. In Third World countries whose poverty has often been attributed to "exploitation" by Western nations, it is not uncommon for those indigenous people most in contact with Westerners in port cities and other places to be visibly less poor than indigenous people out in the hinterlands remote from Western contacts or influence.[42]

To think of some people as simply being higher achievers than others, for whatever reason, is a threat to today's prevailing vision, for it implicitly places the onus on the lagging group to achieve more— and, perhaps more important, deprives the intelligentsia of their role of fighting on the side of the angels against the forces of evil. The very concept of achievement fades into the background, or disappears completely, in some of the verbal formulations of the intelligentsia, where those who turn out to be more successful *ex post* are depicted as having been "privileged" *ex ante*.

How far this vision can depart from reality was shown by a report titled *Ethno-Racial Inequality in the City of Toronto*, which said, "the Japanese are among the most privileged groups in the city"[43] because they were more successful economically than either the other minorities there or the white majority. What makes this conclusion grotesque is a documented history of anti-Japanese discrimination in Canada,[44] where people of Japanese ancestry were interned during the Second World War longer than Japanese Americans were.

Similarly, members of the Chinese minority in Malaysia have been characterized as having "privilege" and the Malay majority as being "deprived," despite a history of official preferential treatment of Malays, going all the way back to British colonial days, when the government provided free education to Malays but the Chinese had to get their own.[45] There is no question that the Chinese greatly *outperformed* the Malays, both in education and in the economy— an inconvenient fact evaded by the rhetoric of privilege and deprivation.

Efforts of the intelligentsia to downplay or discredit achievement by verbally transforming it into "privilege" are by no means confined to the case of the Japanese minority in Canada or the Chinese minority in Malaysia. In many countries around the world, the abandoning or discrediting of the concept of achievement leads to blaming higher achieving groups for the fact that other groups are lower achievers, putting the anointed in the familiar role of being on the side of the angels— and putting many societies on the road to racial or ethnic polarization, and sometimes on the road to ruin. In many places around the world, groups who co-existed peacefully for generations have turned violently against one another when both circumstances and verbally and politically skilled "leaders" appeared at the same time, creating a "perfect storm" of polarization. Intellectuals often help create a climate of opinion in which such perfect storms can occur.

The ego stakes of intellectuals discussing racial issues have led not only to formulating these issues in ways that promote moral melodramas, starring themselves on the side of the angels, but also promoting the depiction of those designated as victims as being people who are especially worthy— the noble oppressed. Thus, much sympathy was generated for the many minority groups in the Habsburg and Ottoman Empires that were dismantled in the wake of Woodrow Wilson's doctrine of the "self-determination" of peoples. But the newly created or newly reconstituted nations carved out of these dismantled empires quickly became places marked by the newly empowered minorities oppressing other minorities in the nations now ruled by the erstwhile minorities of the Habsburg or Ottoman Empires. However, these new oppressions seldom attracted much attention from intellectuals who had championed the cause of the Habsburg or Ottoman minorities who were now the new oppressors.

Something similar has happened in the United States, where intellectuals who protested racism against blacks have seldom criticized anti-Semitism or anti-Asian words and deeds among black Americans. The beating up of Asian American school children by black classmates in New York and Philadelphia, for example, has been going on for years,[46] and yet has attracted little attention, much less criticism, from the intelligentsia. Contrary to visions conjured up by some of the intelligentsia, suffering oppression does not make people noble, nor necessarily even tolerant. Moreover, the behavior of the intelligentsia often reflects a pattern in which principles are less important than fashions— and Asian Americans are not in vogue.

There have also been random outbursts of violence by young blacks against whites in various cities across the United States, but these attacks are either not reported in much of the media or else the racial basis for these attacks on strangers is ignored or downplayed, even when the attackers accompany their attacks with anti-white invective.[47]

Chapter 5

Race and Intelligence

There are few, if any, issues more explosive than the question of whether there are innate differences in intelligence among the various races. Here it is especially important to be clear as to what is meant, and not meant, by "intelligence" in this context. What is *not* meant are wisdom, skills or even developed mental capabilities in general. Virtually everyone recognizes that these things depend to some extent on circumstances, including upbringing in general and education in particular. Those on both sides of the question of race and intelligence are arguing about something much more fundamental— the innate potential for thinking, the ability to grasp and manipulate complex concepts, without regard to whatever judgment may or may not have been acquired from experience or upbringing.

This has sometimes been called *native* intelligence— the mental capacity with which one was born— but it could more aptly be called the mental *potential* at the time of conception, since the development of the brain can be affected by what happens in the womb between conception and birth. These things can happen differently according to the behavior of the mother, including diet, smoking and intake of alcohol and narcotics, not to mention damage that can occur to the brain during its passage through the birth canal. Genetic mental potential would therefore mean the potential at the moment of conception, rather than at birth, since "native intelligence" has already been affected by environment.

Similarly, if one is comparing the innate potential of races, rather than individuals, then that innate potential as it existed at the dawn of the human species may be different from what it is today, since all races have been subjected to various environmental conditions that can affect what kinds of individuals are more likely or less likely to survive and leave offspring to carry on their family line and the race. Large disparities in the geographic, historic, economic and social conditions in which different races developed for centuries open the possibility that different kinds of individuals have had different probabilities of surviving and flourishing in these different environmental conditions. No one knows if this is true— and this is just one of the many things that no one knows about race and intelligence.

The ferocity of the assertions on both sides of this issue seems to reflect the ideological importance of the dispute— that is, how it affects the vision and the agendas of intellectuals. During the Progressive era, assertions of innate racial differences in intelligence were the basis for proposing sweeping interventions to keep certain races from entering the country and to suppress the reproduction of particular races already living within the country. During the later twentieth century, assertions of innate equality of the races became the basis for proposing sweeping interventions whenever there were substantial statistical differences among the races in incomes, occupational advances and other social outcomes, since such disparities have been regarded as presumptive evidence of discrimination, given the presumed innate equality of the races themselves.

Innate intellectual ability, however, is just one of the many factors that can cause different groups to have different outcomes, whether these are groups that differ by race, sex, religion, nationality or the many other subdivisions of the human species. In short, innate equality of intellectual potential in races, even if it could be proven, would not prove that their differences in outcomes could only be a result of their being treated differently by others— given the many geographic, demographic and other influences affecting the development of intellectual potential into concrete capabilities among individuals and races.

Even if there are no innate restrictions on the range of intelligence among individuals from different races, this is not to say that there can be no induced differences in *average* mental potential or average developed capabilities in a given race, whether induced by differential reproduction rates between different social classes within a given race in a given environment or by other influences. What is also important to keep in mind is the question of both the magnitude and the duration of whatever differences in either intellectual potential or developed capabilities that may exist as of a given time. These and other possibilities need to be examined separately, empirically— and carefully.

HEREDITY AND ENVIRONMENT

In principle, all the factors affecting intelligence can be dichotomized into those due to heredity and all the remaining influences, which can be put into the category of environment. However, life does not always cooperate with our analytical categories. If environment can affect which hereditary traits are more likely to survive, then these two categories are no longer hermetically sealed off from one another.

If, for example, we take some characteristic that is widely agreed to be affected primarily by genetics— height, for example— it has been argued that the average height of Frenchmen has been lowered by massive casualties in war, as a result of the decimations of French soldiers during the Napoleonic wars or during the First World War, or both, since the biggest and strongest men have been more likely to have been taken into the military forces and sent into battle. Thus two races with initially identical genetic potential for height can end up with different heights, and different genetic potentials for height in future generations, if one race has been subjected more often to conditions more likely to kill off tall people at an early age, before they reproduce sufficiently to replace their numbers and maintain their share of their race's gene pool.

Similarly, some have sought to explain the over-representation of Jews among people with high intellectual achievements by differential survival rates within the Jewish population. It would be hard to think of any other group subjected to such pervasive and relentless persecution, for thousands of years, as the Jews. Such persecutions, punctuated from time to time by mass lethal violence, obviously reduced Jews' survival prospects. According to this hypothesis, if people of only average or below average intelligence were less likely to survive millennia of such persecutions, then— regardless of Jews' initial genetic intellectual potential— a disproportionate share of those who survived physically, and especially of those who could survive *as Jews*, without converting to another religion to escape persecution, were likely to be among the more ingenious.

Despite a tendency to think of heredity and environment as if they were mutually exclusive and jointly exhaustive, there are many other ways in which environment can change heredity, so that races that may have initially had the same genetic potential for intelligence can end up with different genetic potentials, as a result of their different environments.

Widely available subsidies for individuals who are less successful economically— who, as a group, may average lower IQs than very successful individuals— can lead to an increase in the number of babies born to teenage dropouts, for example, while higher rates of taxation of individuals with higher levels of education and higher earnings can lead to the latter having fewer children than otherwise, as a result of their unwillingness to produce more offspring, whose chances of getting the amount and quality of education required to maintain the living standards into which they were born would be reduced if their parents' income and time were spread out over a larger number of children. If both sets of individuals and families are of the same race, then the average intelligence of that race could be reduced— not only in the next generation, but in subsequent generations as well, since a larger portion of the offspring of that race would be supplied by the less successful members than if such policies of subsidies and taxes did not exist.

Even if races, as such, did not initially have different genetic potential, the fact that the genes of less successful members of a particular race become a growing proportion of all the genes passed on to subsequent generations can reduce the *average* hereditary potential of the race as a whole, in much the same way that environmental factors can reduce heights, not only in the next generation, but in subsequent generations as well. Two different kinds of environment can influence such an outcome: (1) an external environment which produces various activities of both governmental and non-governmental organizations to subsidize a counterproductive lifestyle and (2) an internal culture in which large numbers of members of a particular racial or ethnic group are willing to live on the dole and spare themselves the efforts required to rise to economic independence.

This second requirement, without which the first may not do nearly as much damage, may be entirely environmental, but it can be no less damaging to the race and to the composition of its pool of genes. The same subsidies may be available to everyone below a specified income level but, if some racial or ethnic groups are from a culture that refuses to adopt a lifestyle of dependency, then these groups escape both the immediate and the longer-run consequences of that lifestyle. Here a crucial distinction must be made between environment conceived as the immediate surroundings and environment conceived as including a cultural heritage which can differ greatly between contemporary groups living at similar socioeconomic levels and facing the same objective opportunities in schools and in the economy.

Whether or not this hypothesis can be validated by empirical research, like the hypothesis about the heights of Frenchmen it demonstrates that heredity theories and environmental theories of group differences are not hermetically sealed off from one another, since environment can influence the survival rate of hereditary characteristics. Moreover, the question of *average* mental potential or average developed mental capabilities between races is different from the question whether some races have a limited *range* of mental abilities— a ceiling on their intellectual potential that is lower than for some other races, as implied by genetic determinists of the Progressive era.

While the average Frenchman may not be as tall as the average American, Charles DeGaulle was much taller than most Americans. There is similarly no reason why differences in average IQs between any two groups— racial or otherwise— need to imply that high IQs cannot be achieved by members of both groups. These are questions to be answered empirically. These are also questions relevant to assertions by people like Madison Grant and others in the Progressive era that whole races must be severely restricted in their reproduction or, in Sir Francis Galton's words, require "the gradual extinction of an inferior race."[1]

Heredity and environment can interact in many ways. For example, it is known that children who are the first born have on average higher IQs than their later born siblings.[2] Whatever the reasons for this, if families in group *A* have an average of two children and families in group *B* have an average of six children, then the average IQ in group *A* is likely to be higher than in group *B*— even if the innate genetic potential of the two groups is the same— because half the people in group *A* are first-borns, while only one-sixth of those in group *B* are.

In some cultures, marriage between first cousins is acceptable, or even common, while in other cultures it is taboo. These differences existed long before science discovered the negative consequences of in-breeding— and in some cultures such patterns have continued long after these scientific discoveries. Races, classes or other social groups with very different incest taboos can therefore start out with identical genetic potential and yet end up with different capabilities. The point here is simply that there are too many variables involved for dogmatic pronouncements to be made on either side of the issue of innate equality or innate inequality of the races as they exist today.

Since there has been no method yet devised to measure the innate potential of individuals at the moment of conception, much less the innate potential of races at the dawn of the human species, the prospect of a definitive answer to the question of the relationship of race and innate mental ability seems remote, if possible at all.

Put differently, the utter certainty of many who have answered this question in one way or in the opposite way seems premature at best, when all that we have at this point, when it comes to race and intelligence, is a small island of knowledge in a vast sea of the unknown. However, neither certainty nor precision have been necessary for making practical decisions on many other questions, so there needs to be some assessment of the magnitude of what is in dispute and then some assessment of how the evidence bears on that practical question.

THE MAGNITUDES IN QUESTION

The genetic determinists of the late nineteenth and early twentieth centuries asserted not merely that there were differences in the average mental capacity of different races, but also that these differences were of a magnitude sufficient to make it urgent to at least reduce the reproduction of some races, as people like Margaret Sanger and Madison Grant suggested, or even to promote "the gradual extinction of an inferior race"[3] as Sir Francis Galton advocated. The mental test scores of that era, which seemed to support not merely a difference in intellectual capacity between races but a difference of a sufficient magnitude to make drastic actions advisable, have since then been shown empirically to be far from having the permanence that was once assumed.

Both the magnitude and the permanence of racial differences on mental tests have been undermined by later empirical research, quite aside from questions about the validity of such tests. As regards magnitude, Professor Arthur R. Jensen of the University of California at Berkeley, whose research published in 1969 reopened the question of racial differences in mental capacity and set off a storm of controversy,[4] provided an insight that is especially salient, since he has been prominent, if not pre-eminent, among contemporaries on the side of hereditary theories of intelligence:

> When I worked in a psychological clinic, I had to give individual intelligence tests to a variety of children, a good many of whom came from an impoverished background. Usually I felt these children were really brighter than their IQ would indicate. They often appeared inhibited in their responsiveness in the testing situation on their first visit to my office, and when this was the case I usually had them come in on two to four different days for half-hour sessions with me in a "play therapy" room, in which we did nothing more than get better acquainted by playing ball, using finger paints, drawing on the blackboard, making things out of clay, and so forth. As soon as the child seemed to be completely at home in this setting, I would retest him on a parallel form of the Stanford-Binet. A boost in IQ of 8 to 10 points or so was the rule; it rarely failed, but neither was the gain very often much above this.[5]

Since "8 to 10 points" is more than half the average IQ difference of 15 points between black and white Americans, the disappearance of that much IQ differential from a simple change of immediate circumstances suggests that the magnitude of what is in question today is *not* whether some people are capable only of being "hewers of wood and drawers of water." Professor Jensen's conclusions on a practical level are therefore very different from the conclusions of Margaret Sanger, Madison Grant or Sir Francis Galton in earlier years:

Whenever we select a person for some special educational purpose, whether for special instruction in a grade-school class for children with learning problems, or for a "gifted" class with an advanced curriculum, or for college attendance, or for admission to graduate training or a professional school, we are selecting an *individual*, and we are selecting him and dealing with him as an individual for reasons of his individuality. Similarly, when we employ someone, or promote someone in his occupation, or give some special award or honor to someone for his accomplishments, we are doing this to an individual. The variables of social class, race, and national origin are correlated so imperfectly with any of the valid criteria on which the above decisions should depend, or, for that matter, with any behavioral characteristic, that these background factors are irrelevant as a basis for dealing with individuals— as students, as employees, as neighbors. Furthermore, since, as far as we know, the full range of human talents is represented in all the major races of man and in all socioeconomic levels, it is unjust to allow the mere fact of an individual's racial or social background to affect the treatment accorded to him.[6]

Nor was Arthur R. Jensen as confident as the writers of the Progressive era had been about the meaning of a mental test score. Professor Jensen said he had "very little confidence in a single test score, especially if it is the child's first test and more especially if the child is from a poor background and of a different race from the examiner."[7] He also acknowledged the possible effect of home environment. Professor Jensen pointed out that "3 out of 4 Negroes failing the Armed Forces Qualification Test come from families of four or more children."[8] In other words, he saw that more than race was involved.

Jensen's article, which renewed a controversy that has since lasted for decades, was titled "How Much Can We Boost IQ and Scholastic Achievement?" His answer— long since lost in the storms of controversies that followed— was that scholastic achievement could be much improved by different teaching methods, but that these different teaching methods were not likely to change IQ scores much.[9]

Far from concluding that lower IQ groups were not educable, Jensen said: "One of the great and relatively untapped reservoirs of mental ability in the disadvantaged, it appears from our research, is the basic ability to learn. We can do more to marshal this strength for educational purposes."[10] He argued for educational reforms, saying that "scholastic performance— the acquisition of the basic skills— can be boosted much more, at least in the early years, than can the IQ" and that, among "the disadvantaged," there are "high school students who have failed to learn basic skills which they could easily have learned many years earlier" if taught in different ways.[11]

As someone writing against a later orthodoxy— one in which only such non-genetic factors as test bias and social environment were acceptable as factors behind racial differences in IQ scores— Jensen confronted not only opposing beliefs, but also a dogmatism about those beliefs reminiscent of the opposite dogmatism of genetic determinists of an earlier time. Professor Jensen wrote in 1969: "A preordained, doctrinaire stance with regard to this issue hinders the achievement of a scientific understanding of the problem. To rule out of court, so to speak, any reasonable hypotheses on purely ideological grounds is to argue that static ignorance is preferable to increasing our knowledge of reality."[12]

Jensen was also concerned with social consequences, as well as with questions of scientific findings. He pointed out that "Negro middle- and upper-class families have fewer children than their white counterparts, while Negro lower-class families have more," and that these facts "have some relationship to intellectual ability," as shown by the disproportionate representation of blacks from large families among those who failed the Armed Forces Qualification Test. He said that "current welfare policies"— presumably because they subsidized the birth of more children by black lower-class families— could lead to negative effects on black educational achievement. Jensen concluded that these welfare policies and "the possible consequences of our failure seriously to study these questions may well be viewed by future generations as our society's greatest injustice to Negro Americans."[13]

To argue, as Professor Jensen has, that environment can have detrimental effects on the *average* hereditary endowment of a race is not to say, as Madison Grant did, that "race is everything" or to say, as Francis Galton did, that "the gradual extinction of an inferior race" is the only solution for those races whose intellectual potential must be written off. Both Grant and Galton argued as if there is some inherent ceiling to the intelligence of some races— not simply that differential survival rates of people of the same race with different IQs can statistically lower the average IQ, even though the IQ *range* for individuals of that race may go as high as that of other individuals from other races.

While controversies about race and IQ focus on explanations for the differences in median IQs among groups, the magnitude of those differences is also crucial. Research by Professor James R. Flynn, an American expatriate in New Zealand, concluded that the average IQ of Chinese Americans in 1945 to 1949 was 98.5, compared to a norm of 100 for whites.[14] Even if we were to arbitrarily assume, for the sake of argument— as Professor Flynn did *not*— that this difference at that time was due solely to genetics, the magnitude of the difference would hardly justify the kinds of drastic policies advocated by eugenicists.

In reality, the occupational achievements of both Chinese Americans and Japanese Americans exceed those of white Americans with the same IQs. Japanese Americans were found to have occupational achievements equal to that of those whites who had 10 points higher IQs than themselves, and Chinese Americans to have occupational achievements equal to those of those whites who had 20 points higher IQs than themselves.[15]

In short, even though much research has shown that IQ differences matter for educational, occupational and other achievements,[16] the magnitude of those differences also matters, and in particular cases other factors may outweigh IQ differences in determining outcomes. Incidentally, other IQ studies at different times and places show people of Chinese and Japanese ancestry with *higher* IQs than whites,[17] though the differences are similarly small in these studies as well.

The importance of other factors besides IQ is not a blank check for downplaying or disregarding mental test scores when making employment, college admissions or other decisions. Although empirical evidence shows that Chinese Americans and Japanese Americans tend to perform better in educational institutions than whites with the same mental test scores as themselves, other empirical evidence shows that blacks tend to perform *below* the level of those whites with the *same* test scores as themselves.[18] Clearly, then, with blacks as with Chinese and Japanese Americans, *other* factors besides IQs have a significant influence on actual educational outcomes, even though these other factors operate in a different direction for different groups.

None of this means that mental tests— whether IQ tests, college aptitude tests, or others— can be disregarded when it comes to making practical decisions about individuals, even if they do not justify sweeping inferences about genes or discrimination. When deciding whom to hire, admit to college or select for other kinds of endeavors, the relevant question about tests is: What has been the track record of a particular test in predicting subsequent performances— both absolutely and in comparison with alternative criteria? It is essentially an empirical statistical question, rather than a matter of speculation or ideology.

The issue is not even whether the particular questions in the test seem plausibly relevant to the endeavor at hand, as even courts of law have misconceived the issue.[19] If knowing fact *A* enables you to make predictions about outcome *B* with a better track record than alternative criteria, then plausibility is no more relevant than it was when wine experts dismissed Professor Orley Ashenfelter's use of weather statistics to predict wine prices— which predictions turned out to have a better track record than the methods used by wine experts.[20]

PREDICTIVE VALIDITY

Even if IQ tests or college admissions tests do not accurately measure the "real" intelligence of prospective students or employees— however "real" intelligence might be defined— the practical question is whether whatever they do measure is correlated with future success in the particular endeavor. Despite numerous claims that mental tests under-estimate the "real" intelligence of blacks, a huge body of research has demonstrated repeatedly that the future scholastic performances of blacks are *not* under-estimated by these tests which tend, if anything, to predict a slightly higher performance level than that which actually follows, contrary to the situation with Chinese Americans or Japanese Americans. While blacks tend to score lower than whites on a variety of aptitude, academic achievement and job tests, empirical evidence indicates that those whites with the *same* test scores as blacks have, on average, a track record of higher subsequent performances than blacks, whether academically or on the job. This includes academic performance in colleges, law schools, and medical schools, and job performance in the civil service and in the Air Force.[21]

Nor is this pattern unique to American blacks. In the Philippines, for example, students from low-income and rural backgrounds have not only had lower than average test scores, but have also done worse academically at the University of the Philippines than other students with the *same* low test scores as themselves.[22] In Indonesia, where men have averaged lower test scores than women, men with the same test scores as women have done poorer academic work than women at the University of Indonesia.[23]

A long-range study by Lewis Terman, beginning in 1921, followed children with IQs of 140 and above in their later lives and found that those children who came from homes where the parents were less educated, and were from a lower socioeconomic level, did not achieve prominence in their own lives as often as other children in the same IQ range who had the further advantage of coming from homes with a higher cultural level.[24] In short, other factors besides those captured by IQ tests affect performances in various endeavors— and affect them differently for different groups. But one cannot just arbitrarily wave test results aside, in order to get more demographic "representation" of racial or other groups with lower test scores as employees, students or in other contexts.

A growing body of empirical data shows that black students mismatched with the particular colleges or universities they attend fail or drop out more often than other students at those institutions— and more often than black students with the same test scores or other academic qualifications as themselves who attend academic institutions where the other students are on a similar academic level.[25] The problem is *not* that these black students are "unqualified" to be in a college or university. They may be highly qualified to be in some college or university, but are mismatched with the particular college or university that has admitted them for the sake of demographic "diversity" by disregarding test scores and other academic qualifications.

A study at M.I.T., for example, showed that the average black student there had math SAT scores in the top 10 percent nationwide— and in the bottom 10 percent at M.I.T. Nearly one-fourth of these extraordinarily high-ranking black students failed to graduate from M.I.T.[26] More generally, students with a given mathematics level succeeded in getting science, technology, engineering and mathematics degrees more often at academic institutions where the other students were at comparable academic levels.[27]

It has been much the same story in law schools. At the Georgetown University Law School, for example, the median test score of black students on the Law School Aptitude Test was at the 75th percentile— hardly "unqualified"— but that score was lower than the score of *any* white student admitted to this elite law school at the same time.[28] Studies at a number of law schools indicate that black students admitted with lower qualifications than other students not only do less well academically while in law school but fail the bar examination more often than either the white students at their law school or black students with the same academic qualifications as themselves who attend law schools where the other students have academic qualifications similar to their own.[29]

In short, ignoring test scores and other academic qualifications when admitting minority students turns minority students with all the qualifications for success into artificially induced failures, by mismatching them with the institutions that admit them under lower standards.

ABSTRACT QUESTIONS

A common finding among groups with low mental test scores, in various countries around the world, has been an especial lack of interest and proficiency in answering abstract questions. A study in England, for example, showed that rural working class boys trailed their urban peers more on abstract questions than on other kinds of questions.[30] In the Hebrides Islands off Scotland, where the average IQ of the Gaelic-speaking children was 85— the same as that among blacks in the United States— the Gaelic-speaking youngsters did well on informational items but trailed their English-speaking peers most on items involving such abstractions as time, logic, and other non-verbal factors.[31] In Jamaica, where IQs averaged below normal, the lowest performance was on the least verbal test.[32] A 1932 study of white children living in isolated mountain communities in the United States showed that they not only had low IQ scores over all, but were especially deficient on questions involving abstract comprehension.[33]

Indian children being tested in South Africa were likewise reported as showing a "lack of interest in non-verbal materials."[34] Lower class youngsters in Venezuela were described as "non-starters" on one of the well-known abstract tests used there.[35] Inhabitants of the Hebrides likewise gave evidence of not being fully oriented toward such questions.[36] Black American soldiers tested during the First World War tended to "lapse into inattention and almost into sleep" during abstract tests, according to observers.[37]

That black-white mental test score differences in America are likewise greatest on abstract questions[38] is hardly surprising, in view of this common pattern among groups that score low in various countries around the world, regardless of the race of the particular group. But the fact that low-scoring groups tend to do their worst on abstract questions is also contrary to the claim made by some critics of mental tests that group differences in scores on these tests are due primarily to the words used in these tests or to the culturally loaded subjects in the questions. However, an interest in abstractions is itself something characteristic of particular cultures and not of others. When H.H. Goddard said of the immigrants he tested at Ellis Island that they "cannot deal with abstractions,"[39] he overlooked the possibility that they had no real interest in abstractions.

Even if those who take mental tests try to do their best on abstract questions, as on other questions, a lifetime of disinterest in such things can mean that their best is not very good, even if that is not due to a lack of innate potential. If Asian American youngsters were to do their best playing basketball against black American youngsters on a given day, their best might not be nearly as good as the best of youngsters who had spent far more time on this activity before. Similarly if black youngsters try their best on a test measuring mental skills that they have not spent as much time developing as Asian youngsters have.

Neither genes nor a biased test is necessary to explain such results. If there were some group which assiduously pursued intellectual development and yet ended up with low IQs, the case for genetic determinism might be overwhelming. But there seems to be no such group anywhere.

If one chooses to call tests that require the mastery of abstractions culturally biased, because some cultures put more emphasis on abstractions than others do, that raises fundamental questions about what the tests are for. In a world where the ability to master abstractions is essential in mathematics, science and other endeavors, the measurement of that ability is not an arbitrary bias. A culture-free test might be appropriate in a culture-free society— but there are no such societies.

Nor is the importance of particular kinds of abilities constant over time, even in the same endeavors. Criteria that might have been suited to selecting individuals to be shepherds or farmers in centuries past may not be adequate for selecting individuals for a different range of occupations today— or even to selecting individuals to be shepherds or farmers today, in an age of scientific agriculture and scientific animal husbandry.

TEST SCORE DIFFERENCES

Whether or not whatever factors make for high or low mental test scores make these tests a good measure of innate mental potential, what matters from a practical standpoint is whether those factors are important in education, in the economy and in life. Disregarding test scores, in order to get a higher demographic "representation" of black students in colleges and universities, for example, has systematically mismatched these students with the particular institutions in which they have been enrolled.

When the top tier colleges and universities accept black students whose test scores are like those of students in the second tier of academic institutions, then those colleges and universities in the second tier, which now find themselves with a smaller pool of black applicants whose qualifications are suited to their institutions, are thus left to accept black students whose test scores are more like those of students in the third tier— and so on down the line. In short, mismatching at the top tier institutions has a domino effect across the field of academic institutions, leading to far higher rates of academic failure among black students than among other students.

A widely-praised book on the effects of affirmative action in college admissions— *The Shape of the River* by former college presidents William Bowen and Derek Bok— claimed to have refuted this mismatching hypothesis with data showing that black students "graduated at *higher* rates, the more selective the school that they attended" (emphasis in the original).[40] But what would be relevant to testing the mismatching hypothesis is the *difference* in test scores between black and white students at the same institutions— and this difference has been less at Harvard (95 points on the combined SAT test scores) than at Duke (184 points) or Rice (271 points).[41] Other data likewise indicate that black students graduate at a higher rate in colleges where their test scores are more similar to those of white students at the same institutions.[42] As Bowen and Bok themselves say: "There has been a much more pronounced narrowing of the black-white gap in SAT scores among applicants to the most selective colleges."[43]

That the high rate of college dropouts found among black students in general is not as great at institutions where the racial mental test score gap is not as great is a *confirmation* of the mismatching hypothesis that Bowen and Bok claim to have *refuted.* The fact that access to their raw data has been refused to others[44] suggests that the great praise showered on their book in the media may reflect agreement with its message and its vision, rather than a critical examination of its evidence and reasoning.

Although most controversies about racial differences in intelligence focus on *averages*, such as those of IQ scores, what is also relevant is the *range* of these scores. As already noted, much of what was said in the early twentieth century seemed to indicate a belief that there was some ceiling to intelligence that was lower for some races than for others. This was another way in which Professor Jensen differed from early twentieth century believers in genetic determinism, since he acknowledged that "as far as we know, the full range of human talents is represented in all the major races of man."[45]

As for that supposed lower intellectual ceiling, among the "beaten men from beaten races" disdained during the Progressive era were Jews— who were later in the forefront of those whose scientific work made the United

States the first nuclear power, and Jews have been wholly disproportionately represented among Nobel laureates worldwide.[46] International chess championships have been won by any number of members of another group of "beaten men from beaten races," the Slavs— and the first human being to go into space was a Slav. The idea of an intellectual ceiling for particular races seems unsustainable, whatever might be said of intellectual averages.

There have been studies of blacks with IQs significantly above the national average, these studies having lower cutoff IQ scores of 120, 130, and 140.[47] One of these studies turned up a nine-year-old girl "of apparently pure Negro stock" with an IQ of 143 on the Porteus mazes test, 180 on the Otis test and "approximately 200" on the Binet IQ test.[48] If there is an intelligence *ceiling* for blacks, and it is up near an IQ of 200, then its practical significance would be wholly different from what was proclaimed by genetic determinists of the Progressive era, who depicted some races as being unfit for survival in any role above that of the proverbial "hewers of wood and drawers of water." No one of course knows whether there is a racial ceiling on anyone's IQ, much less what that ceiling might be.

Although the most common and most heated controversies about racial differences in IQ have centered on black and white Americans, the singling out of any given racial or ethnic group for comparison with the national average in any country creates an implication of uniqueness that is belied by empirical facts, since the national average itself is simply an amalgam of very different IQ levels among a variety of racial, social, regional and other groups.*

---

* These differences are by no means limited to racial or ethnic groups. In Indonesia, residents of Java score higher than Indonesians living in the outer islands, and women score higher than men. (Robert Klitgaard, *Elitism and Meritocracy in Developing Countries* [Baltimore: Johns Hopkins University Press, 1986], pp. 119, 124.) In China, low-income and rural youngsters score lower on examinations (Ibid., p. 19). First-born children in general tend to score higher on mental tests and to do better in school than later children in the same families. (Lillian Belmont and Francis A. Marolla, "Birth Order, Family Size, and Intelligence," *Science*, December 14, 1973, p. 1096. But see also Phillip R. Kunz and Evan T. Peterson, "Family Size and Academic Achievement of Persons Enrolled in High School and the University," *Social Biology*, December 1973, pp. 454–459; Phillip R. Kunz and Evan T. Peterson, "Family Size, Birth Order, and Academic Achievement," *Social Biology*, Summer 1977, pp. 144–148.)

There is nothing unique about the average black American IQ of 85, compared to a national average of 100. At various times and places, other racial or social groups have had very similar IQs. Studies during the era of mass immigration to the United States in the early twentieth century often found immigrant children from various countries with average IQs in the 80s. A 1923 survey of studies of Italian American IQs, for example, found their average IQ to be 85 in one study, 84 in three studies, 83 in another study and 77.5 in still another study. A 1926 survey of American IQ studies found median IQs of 85.6 for Slovaks, 83 for Greeks, 85 for Poles, 78 for Spaniards, and 84 for Portuguese.[49]

Similar IQs in the 80s have been found among people living in the Hebrides Islands off Scotland and in white mountaineer communities in the United States in the 1930s[50]— both groups being of Nordic extraction, people who were supposed to be intellectually superior, according to Madison Grant and others. A 1962 study of the children of people from India tested in South Africa found them to have a mean IQ of 86.8, the same as that of African children there.[51]

Although mental test pioneer Carl Brigham wrote in 1923 that the Army mental tests during the First World War provided an "inventory" of "mental capacity" with "a scientific basis,"[52] in 1930 he recanted his earlier view that low mental test scores among various immigrant groups in the United States reflected low innate intelligence. He belatedly pointed out in 1930 that many of the immigrant men tested by the Army during the First World War were raised in homes where the language spoken was not English. Although Brigham said in his 1923 book that he and other testers had "demonstrated the accuracy of the combined scale as a measure of the intelligence of the groups under consideration,"[53] he said candidly in his 1930 article that his previous conclusions were— in his own words— "without foundation."[54]

For blacks who took those same tests, their very low level of literacy at the time was likewise a factor to be considered, though few commentators took that into account. One sign of that low level of literacy among black soldiers taking the Army mental tests, and how that affected the results, was that black soldiers were more often able to answer some of the more difficult questions that did not require understanding the meaning of written words than they were able to answer much simpler questions that did.*

In addition, one section of one of the Army tests required information such as the color of sapphires, the location of Cornell University, the profession of Alfred Noyes and the city in which the Pierce Arrow automobile was manufactured.[55] Why blacks would have had any reason to know any of these things at that time is a mystery— and why such questions could be considered measures of either black or white innate intelligence is an even bigger mystery. But here, as in other very different contexts, statistical data that seemed to fit prevailing preconceptions among intellectuals have been accepted and proclaimed, with little or no critical examination.

DURATION OF MENTAL TEST RESULTS

During the Progressive era, one of the strongest arguments advanced for eugenics was that the tendency of people with lower IQs to have larger families would, over time, lead to a decline in the national IQ. But the later

---

* In many parts of the Army Alpha test used during the First World War, the modal score of black soldiers was *zero*— derived by subtracting incorrect answers from correct answers, in order to neutralize the effect of guessing. But the actual intellectual substance of some of these questions involved only knowing that "yes" and "no" were opposites, as were "night" and "day," "bitter" and "sweet" and other similarly extremely easy questions— questions too simple to be missed by anyone who knew what the word "opposite" meant. However, in the Army Beta test, given to soldiers who could not read, some of the questions involved looking at pictures of a pile of blocks and determining how many blocks there were, including blocks that were not visible, but whose presence had to be inferred (and counted) from the shape of the piles. Yet fewer than half of the black soldiers received a score of zero on such questions, which were more intellectually demanding, but did not require the ability to read and understand words. Given the very small quantity and very low quality of education received by that generation of blacks, even those who were technically literate were unlikely to have a large vocabulary of written words, so it is hardly surprising that the completely illiterate black soldiers did better on more challenging questions than did blacks with some ability to read. For details, see Carl Brigham, *A Study of American Intelligence* (Princeton: Princeton University Press, 1923), pp. 16–19, 36–38; [Robert M. Yerkes,] National Academy of Sciences, *Psychological Examining in the United States Army* (Washington: Government Printing Office, 1921), Vol. XV, Part III, pp. 874, 875; Thomas Sowell, "Race and IQ Reconsidered," *Essays and Data on American Ethnic Groups*, edited by Thomas Sowell and Lynn D. Collins (Washington: The Urban Institute, 1978), pp. 226–227.

research of Professor James R. Flynn showed that, in more than a dozen countries around the world, the average performance on IQ tests *rose* substantially— by one standard deviation or more— in a generation or two.[56] Only the fact that IQ tests are repeatedly renormed, in order to keep the average IQ at its definitional level of 100, as the average number of questions answered correctly increased, had concealed this rise— and only the fact that Professor Flynn went back to the original raw scores revealed the facts which the renorming had concealed.

Much has been made of the fact that the average IQ among blacks has remained at about 85 over the generations, suggesting that the tests are measuring an unchanging genetic potential. But the apparent permanence of the performance of black Americans on IQ tests is an artifact of the renorming of those tests. The average number of questions answered correctly on IQ tests by blacks in 2002 would have given them an average IQ of 104 by the norms used in 1947–1948, which is to say, slightly higher than the average performance of Americans in general during the earlier period.[57] In short, the performances of blacks on IQ tests have risen significantly over time, just as the performances of other people in the United States and in other countries have, even though the renorming of those tests concealed these changes. While the persistence of a gap between blacks and whites in America on IQ tests leads some to conclude that genetic differences are the reason, the large changes in IQ test performance by both black and white Americans, as well as by the populations of other whole nations around the world, undermine the notion that IQ tests measure an unchanging genetic potential.

The fervor and persistence of the racial IQ debate cannot be assumed to be a measure of its practical implications,* as distinguished from its ideological importance for competing social visions. As already noted, even the leading advocate of genetic theories of IQ differences, Professor Arthur R. Jensen, has seen scholastic achievement as amenable to different teaching

---

* Anyone with experience teaching in American schools or colleges may well question whether either the average black or white student is working so close to his or her ultimate mental capacity as to make that ultimate capacity a matter of practical concern.

methods and has treated IQ differences as an over-estimate of differences in intelligence between children from lower socioeconomic classes and others. Since concrete capabilities matter much more in the real world than do abstract potentialities, educational outcomes are the practical issue, however much this practical issue has been overshadowed by ideological issues.

The leading scholar in the opposing, environmentalist school of thought, Professor James R. Flynn, expressed the narrowness of the practical issues in 2008:

> The race and IQ debate has raged for almost forty years. I have been entangled in it for thirty years. It has been a constant and unwelcome companion, rather like living with an uncongenial spouse from an arranged marriage. It has occupied the time of legions of scholars and laid waste acres of trees. Will we ever see the end of it? At least the debate is entering a new and more sophisticated stage. Given the relatively high values for black IQ in infancy and age 4, the focus should now be on whatever causes the decline of black IQ (compared to white) with age. If that can be settled, the main event will be over.[58]

Professor Flynn has argued that the culture in which most black Americans grow up has had a negative effect on their intellectual development. He pointed out that the offspring of black and white American soldiers, who fathered children with German women during the American occupation of Germany after the Second World War, had no such IQ differences as that among black and white children in the United States. Professor Flynn concluded that the reason for results being different in Germany was that the offspring of black soldiers in Germany "grew up in a nation with no black subculture."[59]

There is other evidence that the black subculture has a negative effect on intellectual achievement. An empirical study published by the National Bureau of Economic Research found that "a higher percentage of Black schoolmates has a strong adverse effect on achievement of Blacks and, moreover, that the effects are highly concentrated in the upper half of the ability distribution."[60] In other words, brighter black students do not perform as well in settings where there are many other black students around them, contrary to the theory that what is needed in educational institutions is some larger "critical mass" of black students, in order to make them feel socially comfortable and thus able to do their best work academically. Yet the unsubstantiated "critical mass" theory has flourished from academic journals to Supreme Court briefs.[61]

Another study, focussing on the effect of ability-grouping on the performances of students in general, mentioned among its conclusions: "Schooling in a homogeneous group of students appears to have a positive effect on high-ability students' achievements, and even stronger effects on the achievements of high-ability minority youth."[62] In other words, high-ability minority youngsters do better in classes that are *intellectually* homogeneous, rather than racially homogeneous, or in which there are many members of their own race.

The negative effects of the black subculture on intellectual development are manifested in other ways as well. A study of high-IQ black adults found that they described their childhoods as "extremely unhappy" more often than other blacks.[63] This study was done long before the current reports of academically striving black students being accused by their peers of "acting white." Empirical studies during this later era show a negative correlation between black students' academic achievement and their popularity among other black students. An opposite pattern was found among white Americans and Asian Americans.[64] In England, lower-class whites show a pattern strikingly similar to that among American blacks who resent academically achieving classmates. British physician Theodore Dalrymple reports lower class school children being beaten up so badly by their lower class classmates as to require hospital treatment, simply because they are doing well in school.[65]

There is other evidence against the "critical mass" theory. In earlier times, from 1892 to 1954, all-black Dunbar High School in Washington sent 34 graduates to Amherst College, usually very few at any given time, and certainly nothing that could be called a "critical mass." Seventy-four percent of those black students graduated from Amherst, 28 percent of these graduating as Phi Beta Kappas.[66] Dunbar did not promote a black subculture. As Senator Edward Brooke, one of its alumni, put it:

> Negro History Week was observed, and in American history they taught about the emancipation of the slaves and the struggle for equality and civil rights. But there was no demand by students for more, no real

interest in Africa and its heritage. We knew about Africa as we knew about Finland.[67]

Yet the "critical mass" theory continues to flourish, with no evidence behind it, but with a peer consensus among the intelligentsia, which is apparently sufficient for many.

The cultural explanation of black-white IQ differences is also consistent with the fact that very young black American children do not lag behind very young white American children on mental tests, but that the gap begins and widens as they grow up. Research as far back as the 1920s found this pattern, as Otto Klineberg reported in a 1941 summary:

> A study by Lacy, for example, showed that the average I.Q. of colored children dropped steadily from 99 to 87 in the first four school grades, whereas the White I.Q. remained almost stationary. Wells also noted that Negro children were equal to Whites at ages six, seven and eight; only slightly inferior at ages nine, ten and eleven; and showed a progressively more marked inferiority from the ages of twelve to sixteen.[68]

Professor Jensen offers an alternative, genetic explanation for this pattern,[69] but a similar pattern was also found among low-IQ European immigrant groups in studies in 1916 to 1920, and among white American children in isolated mountain communities studied in 1930 and 1940,[70] so it is not a racial peculiarity in a genetic sense. Professor Flynn's explanation of this same pattern is consistent with the data cited by Klineberg. But these data are completely inconsistent with the prevailing multiculturalists' doctrine that all cultures are equal. Flynn's cultural explanation of black-white differences in IQ is also consistent with the otherwise puzzling anomaly that the mental test scores of white soldiers from various Southern states during the First World War were lower than the mental test scores of black soldiers from various Northern states at that time.[71]

Striking differences between the regional cultures of the South and the North in times past have been noted by many, including Alexis de Tocqueville, Frederick Law Olmsted and Hinton Helper in the nineteenth century, and Gunnar Myrdal in the twentieth century.[72] Moreover, those differences went back for centuries, when similar differences existed in different regions of Britain, among people who would later settle in the American South and others who would later settle in New England.[73]

Some of these cultural differences have been detailed in *Cracker Culture* by Grady McWhiney and in *Albion's Seed* by David Hackett Fischer, as well as in my book *Black Rednecks and White Liberals*. The fact that whites who came out of that Southern culture scored lower on mental tests than Northern whites— as well as whites from some Southern states scoring lower than blacks from some Northern states— is much more difficult to reconcile with genetic theories than with cultural explanations. In fact, neither of the two main explanations of mental test score differences by the twentieth century intelligentsia— genetic differences or racial discrimination— can account for white Southerners scoring low on the Army mental tests in the First World War. But the cultural explanation is consistent with both blacks and Southern whites scoring low on these tests at that time.

Much has changed in the South in later generations, and especially in the latter decades of the twentieth century, in part as a result of interregional migrations which have changed the demographic and cultural makeup of the South, perhaps more so than other regions of the country. However, as late as the middle of the twentieth century, most blacks in America had been born in the old South, even when they lived in the North, so the culture of the South, which Gunnar Myrdal saw as common to both blacks and whites born in that region, lived on in black ghettos across the country.[74] Many features of that culture have continued to live on today, often insulated from change by being regarded as a sacrosanct part of black culture and identity.

There is another striking phenomenon which cannot be explained by either the hereditary or the environmental theory of IQ differences— as heredity and environment are usually conceived. That is the fact that females are several times as numerous as males among blacks with high IQs,[75] despite the fact that black males and black females inherit the same genes and are raised in the same homes and neighborhoods. Yet a cultural explanation seems more consistent with these findings as well, since the particular culture in which most blacks have lived for centuries, like the culture of white Southerners in the past, has emphasized especially macho roles for males.* It is hardly surprising if such a culture inhibited the intellectual development of both blacks and whites— especially males— in the South.

Further evidence that the male-female difference in IQs among blacks is cultural is that black orphans raised by white families show no such female superiority in IQs, in addition to both sexes having higher average IQs than other black children.[76] It should also be noted that the male-female difference in *average* IQs among blacks is only a few points but, due to the characteristics of a bell curve, a small difference in average IQs translates into a large difference in male-female representation at high IQ levels. Since these high IQ levels are common among students at elite colleges and among people in elite occupations, their impact on demographic representation in such conspicuous places can be considerable.

There is other evidence that "environment" cannot be usefully defined solely in terms of current gross external circumstances, such as income levels or even levels of education. More important, environment cannot be defined solely in terms of surrounding circumstances *at a given time.*

During the era of mass immigration to the United States, for example, it was common for Italian and Jewish children to be raised in similar low-income neighborhoods and to sit side-by-side in the same classrooms. Yet the Jewish children began to improve educationally before the Italian children, who were mostly the offspring of southern Italian parents. Nor was this at all surprising, in light of different cultural attitudes that prevailed

---

* There may be another, but different, environmental reason for the male-female differences in IQs among blacks. There is evidence that females in general are less affected by environmental disadvantages of various sorts than are males. (Arthur R. Jensen, "How Much Can We Boost IQ and Scholastic Achievement?" *Harvard Educational Review*, Winter 1969, pp. 32, 67.) This possibility is independent of the peculiarities of the culture of the South and would apply to other groups with a very different culture, but who have low IQs for other reasons. Which factor carries more weight is hard to determine. Since there was no mass mental testing of white Southern females during the era when there was mass mental testing of white Southern males in the U.S. Army, we have no way to know whether there was a similar IQ difference between the sexes in the white Southern population at that time. However, there are data on sex differences between males and females among Jews, back during the early twentieth century, when Jews scored below average on mental tests. In that era, Jewish girls scored higher than Jewish boys on mental tests. Clifford Kirkpatrick, *Intelligence and Immigration* (Baltimore: The Williams & Wilkins Co., 1926), pp. 26–27.

among Jews and among southern Italians, long before these children were born. Even uneducated Jews respected education, while the imposition of compulsory education in southern Italy was not only resisted but evaded, and in places even led to riots and the burning of school houses.[77] However similar the immediate circumstances of Italian and Jewish school children were on the Lower East Side of New York, each trailed the long shadow of the cultural history and tradition in which they were raised, and those histories and traditions were very different.

Just as the preferences of Progressive-era intellectuals for genetic explanations of group differences led them to give little attention to cultural explanations of intergroup differences in educational achievement, so the preferences of intellectuals in the second half of the twentieth century for external social explanations— racial segregation and/or discrimination in schools being prominent— led them to likewise overlook cultural explanations. But research on a school in a large metropolitan area in the North from 1932 through 1953 found IQ differences between Jewish and Italian children attending that school to be as persistent over the years as black-white IQ differences in racially segregated schools in the South, and IQ differences between Jewish and Puerto Rican youngsters in that same school to be not only as persistent, but as large, as IQ differences between black and white youngsters attending different, racially segregated schools in the Jim Crow-era South.[78]

There were similar IQ differences among Mexican American and Japanese American youngsters living in the same school district out west, at a place and time where there was little occupational difference among their parents.[79] Cultural differences with educational consequences are not peculiar to the United States. When Maori students, admitted under preferential policies at New Zealand's University of Auckland, fail to show up for tutorials as often as other students,[80] their academic failures cannot be attributed automatically to institutional racism or to not having enough "role models"— not if the purpose is to advance Maoris rather than to protect a vision.

It should be noted that an *internal* explanation of racial differences— even if it is cultural, rather than genetic— deprives intellectuals of a moral melodrama and the opportunity that presents to be on the side of the angels against the forces of evil. There are, of course, times to take moral stands on particular issues, but that is very different from saying that issues in general, or racial issues in particular, are to be automatically conceived in ways that create a moral melodrama. Yet internal explanations of economic outcome differences among Americans have become so taboo that it was literally front-page news in the *New York Times* when a conference was held on the possibility that "a culture of poverty" existed, and that this culture helped explain disparate economic and other outcomes among the poor in general or blacks in particular.[81]

Near the end of the twentieth century, another firestorm among the intelligentsia was ignited by the publication of a major study of intelligence testing in general, and the social implications of its results, by Richard J. Herrnstein and Charles Murray, in their book *The Bell Curve*. Although most of the data and analysis in this book dealt with samples of white Americans, its two chapters on ethnic differences in mental test scores dominated discussions of the book, and especially attacks on the book. Yet one of the most important— and most ignored— statements in *The Bell Curve* appears there completely italicized:

> *That a trait is genetically transmitted in individuals does not mean that group differences in that trait are also genetic in origin.*[82]

As an example of that principle, it is known that differences in height among individuals are due mostly to genetics, but the difference in height between the people of North Korea and South Korea cannot be explained that way, because North Koreans were not shorter than South Koreans before drastic differences in living standards between the two halves of Korea began with that country's partitioning after the Second World War,[83] with North Korea being run by a draconian dictatorship that left its people in dire poverty. So, although genetics may explain *most* differences in height among most individuals and groups, it cannot explain *all* differences in height among all groups.

Whether there are, or have been, environmental differences of comparable magnitudes between other groups at various times and places, in ways that would affect mental capabilities, is a question that is open to empirical investigation. But what *The Bell Curve* says about the relative effects of heredity and environment on intergroup differences is that there is simply no foregone conclusion either way— which is the opposite of what was said by most of the intelligentsia in either the Progressive era or the later liberal and multicultural eras.

While *The Bell Curve* says that "the instability of test scores across generations should caution against taking the current ethnic differences as etched in stone,"[84] it also refuses to accept the arguments of those who "deny that genes have *anything* to do with group differences, a much more ambitious proposition."[85] Authors Herrnstein and Murray declared themselves "resolutely agnostic" on the relative weight of heredity and environment in ethnic differences in cognitive abilities, because "the evidence does not yet justify an estimate."[86]

Saying that existing evidence is inadequate to reach sweeping conclusions on a complex question like the existence or non-existence of differences in innate mental potential among races might not seem to be something to stir heated controversies, unless someone can point to definitive evidence, one way or the other, which no one has.* Nevertheless, *The Bell Curve* has been widely treated in the media, and even among many academics, as if it were just a restatement of the arguments of people like Madison Grant, despite the fact that (1) only two of its 22 chapters deal with ethnic differences and (2) their conclusions as to both facts and policies are as different from those of the Progressive era as from those of the later liberal and multicultural eras.

Like James R. Flynn, Herrnstein and Murray mention the fact that the children of black and white soldiers on occupation duty in Germany after the Second World War do not show the same IQ differences found between black and white children in the United States,[87] though Herrnstein and Murray do not discuss it at length or offer any explanation. It is simply part

---

* Even if such definitive evidence were possible, its practical effect would be questionable, given the limited magnitude of the differences in scientific dispute today. If science were to prove, for example, that the innate mental potential of blacks is 5 percent more than that of whites, of what practical value would that be, except to alert us to an even greater waste of potential than we might have thought? But that would tell us nothing about how to stop this waste. Moreover, the practical relevance of concerns about the limits of mental potential seems questionable when it is by no means clear that either black or white American students are operating anywhere close to those limits.

of a general presentation of evidence on both sides of the issue, in a book that refuses to pretend that current knowledge permits a definitive answer that would validate the racial views prevailing among intellectuals in either the Progressive era or the later eras.

Whatever the merits or demerits of *The Bell Curve* in general (which I have discussed elsewhere*), neither seems to explain the heated reactions it has provoked. Perhaps the fact that Herrnstein and Murray publicly discussed the taboo subject of race and IQ at all— and did so without repeating the prevailing social pieties— was what offended many, including many who never read the book. The authors of *The Bell Curve* also did not share the prevailing optimism among people who see an environmental explanation of intergroup differences in cognitive ability as showing such differences to be readily amenable to enlightened social policies. Herrnstein and Murray pointed out that environmental differences among groups are passed on from parents to children, just like genetic differences,[88] so their conception of environment is clearly not limited to current surrounding socioeconomic conditions, but includes the cultural heritage as well. Moreover, they did not see the mental tests which *convey* unwelcome news about intergroup differences in current mental capabilities as being the *cause* of those differences or due to "culture bias" in the tests themselves.

Just as Franz Boas had to argue against the *dogmatism* of the prevailing vision of race among the Progressives in the 1920s, in order to get his empirical evidence to the contrary even considered, so the authors of *The Bell Curve* have had to do the same in a later and supposedly more enlightened time. Even being agnostic about ultimate answers to the very complex questions that they explored was not enough to save them from the wrath of those whose social vision and agenda they undermined.

In an all too familiar pattern, the analysis and evidence in *The Bell Curve* were often side-stepped by critics, who instead attacked its authors as people with unworthy motives. John B. Judis of *The New Republic* dismissed *The Bell Curve* as "a combination of bigotry and of metaphysics," using "linguistic legerdemain."[89] Michael Lind of *Harper's* magazine called it part

---

* My comments on both can be found in the essay "Ethnicity and IQ" in *The Bell Curve Wars*, edited by Steven Fraser (New York: Basic Books, 1995), pp. 70–79.

of an "astonishing legitimation" of "a body of racialist pseudoscience" representing "a right-wing backlash," and "covert appeals to racial resentments on the part of white Americans."[90] *Time* magazine called the book a work of "dubious premises and toxic conclusions."[91] Such arguments without arguments were not confined to the media, but were also used by academics, including a number of well-known Harvard professors.

Professor Randall Kennedy, for example, declared that Herrnstein and Murray were "bankrolled by wealthy supporters of right wing reaction,"[92] as if large-scale research projects of all sorts— including those at Harvard— are not bankrolled by somebody and, more fundamentally, as if an arbitrary characterization of those who financed the research says anything about the validity or lack of validity of the work itself. Professor Stephen Jay Gould depicted Herrnstein and Murray as promoting "anachronistic social Darwinism" and "a manifesto of conservative ideology."[93] Professor Henry Louis Gates said that the "most pernicious aspect of Murray and Herrnstein's dismissal of the role of environment" is the implication that social programs to advance blacks are futile,[94] though Professor Gates did not quote anything from *The Bell Curve* to substantiate this claim.

Professor Nathan Glazer likewise questioned "the motivations of the authors"[95] and concluded that, even if Herrnstein and Murray were correct in saying that currently prevailing beliefs are based on an untruth, "I ask myself whether the untruth is not better for American society than the truth."[96]

By falsely portraying the authors of *The Bell Curve* as genetic determinists, and then offering little besides vituperation against them, intellectuals may inadvertently promote the false conclusion that there is no serious argument or evidence against genetic determinism. With certainty remote and the magnitudes now in dispute of questionable social consequence,* the ferocity of the attacks on those who deviate from the prevailing orthodoxy may signal little more than the sanctity of a vision or fear of the truth.

---

* Even though the social consequences of a 15-point intergroup difference in IQ are very significant, what remains in dispute among major contemporary protagonists on opposite sides of the heredity-versus-environment issue is not whether all of that difference is due to genes. Nor is the issue between today's major contending protagonists whether there is a racial ceiling to intelligence, as was once widely assumed among genetic determinists of the early twentieth century. Moreover, the research of Professor James R. Flynn has destroyed the early twentieth century prediction of declining national IQs, while radical changes in the relative rankings of Jews on mental tests between the period of the First World War and their very different rankings in later years undermined belief in the permanence of group and intergroup IQ levels.

Chapter 6

Liberalism and Multiculturalism

No issue in American society in recent times has generated more pious rhetoric, unctuousness, and sheer hypocrisy than race relations and racial problems.

Paul Hollander[1]

Between the earliest years of the twentieth century and the last half of that century, the prevailing ideologies about race among intellectuals did a complete reversal. But, just as there was not simply one view among intellectuals in either period, so there were transitions within both the first half of the century and the second half. The biggest transition during the second half of the twentieth century was the transition to what can be called the liberal era on race in the United States, which in turn metamorphosed into the multicultural era. Moreover, such transitions were not confined to the United States, but were common in Western civilization, whether in Europe, the Western Hemisphere or Australia and New Zealand. In both the liberal and the multicultural eras, the issue of "racial justice" loomed large, though the meaning of that term changed over time, as well as differing among different intellectuals at the same time.

THE LIBERAL ERA

Just as the horrors of the First World War led to an about-face among Progressives who had before supported overseas expansions that conquered other races during the Spanish-American war and later American interventions in Latin America, as well as the historic intervention in the war raging in Europe, so the horrors of the Second World War— and, more specifically, the Holocaust— led to painful reconsiderations of racial beliefs and policies in the Western world.

This is not to say that there had been no change in attitudes toward race since the Progressive era until the Second World War. A coherent school of thought, opposed to the prevailing Progressive era view of race, emerged in the 1920s under the leadership of anthropologist Franz Boas, a professor at Columbia University, to challenge the Progressive era orthodoxy. Boas and his followers emphasized environmental explanations of racial and ethnic differences, and apparently this approach made some inroads into the way some intellectuals saw race. Some changes were apparent by the 1930s. As already noted, in 1930 Carl Brigham recanted his earlier views on what the Army mental tests implied about the intelligence of men of various ethnicities.

As the Jewish population in America, whom Brigham had especially singled out for their low scores on Army mental tests during the First World War, became more assimilated and more educated, later mental test studies usually showed them doing far better than on the Army tests— and better than the American population as a whole.[2]

By the 1930s, the climate of opinion had changed sufficiently that Madison Grant's last book, *The Conquest of a Continent*, was panned by reviewers and *Clashing Tides of Color* by his prize pupil, Lothrop Stoddard, was ridiculed.[3] *The Christian Century* magazine, for example, said of Grant's book: "It gave to prejudice and hatred the false rationalization of an argument having the form, if not the substance, of science."[4] A 1934 survey of opinions among psychologists found 25 percent still believing that blacks had innately inferior intelligence, while 11 percent believed that blacks had equal intelligence and 64 percent believed the data to be inconclusive.[5]

What had eroded were not only the particular beliefs of the Progressive era but also the dogmatic tone of certainty of the Progressives. Otto Klineberg, one of Boas' disciples who promoted the alternative, environmental explanation of mental test differences, did so without the claims of scientific certainty made by Progressives, when he said: "We have no right to conclude that there are no racial differences in mental ability, since it is conceivable that new techniques may some day be developed which will indicate that such differences do exist."[6]

The Liberal Vision

Despite these developments in both beliefs and methods, however, it was the Second World War that marked a decisive turning point in American intellectuals' views of race relations. If there is a single book that might be said to mark that turning point in thinking about race among the intelligentsia, it would be *An American Dilemma* by Swedish economist Gunnar Myrdal, published in 1944. It was a massive study— more than a thousand pages long— of the many aspects of black-white relations in the United States, and its thesis was that American racial policies, especially in the South, marked a glaring contradiction between the nation's fundamental founding principles of freedom and equality and its actual practices as regards blacks. How to resolve that contradiction was the dilemma posed by Myrdal.

By this time, Progressives had begun calling themselves liberals, so this now became the prevailing liberal vision, as it evolved in the second half of the twentieth century.

Broadly speaking, while in the Progressive era socioeconomic differences between races were attributed to race— genetics— in the liberal era such differences between races were often attributed to racism. In neither era were alternative explanations taken seriously by much of the intelligentsia. In the liberal era, attributing any part of the differences between blacks and whites in incomes, crime, education, etc., to internal causes— even if social or cultural, rather than genetic— was often dismissed as "blaming the victim," a phrase preempting the issue rather than debating it.

If heredity was the reigning orthodoxy of the Progressive era, environment became the reigning orthodoxy of the liberal era. Moreover, "environment" usually meant the *external* contemporary environment, rather than including the internal cultural environment of minorities themselves. If minorities were seen as the problem before, the majority was seen as the problem now.

These premises were stated quite clearly in the introduction to *An American Dilemma*, where that dilemma was described as "a white man's problem" and Myrdal added, "little, if anything, could be scientifically explained in terms of the peculiarities of the Negroes themselves."[7] Despite the invocation of science, so reminiscent of the earlier Progressive era intellectuals, this was an arbitrary premise which, if followed consistently, would treat black Americans as simply abstract people with darker complexions, who were victims of what Myrdal called "confused and contradictory attitudes" in the minds of white Americans.[8] Yet Myrdal's own massive study brought out many behavioral and attitudinal differences between blacks and whites, though in the end none of this changed the basic premise of *An American Dilemma*, which remained the central premise of liberal intellectuals for decades thereafter.

This premise— that the racial problem was essentially one inside the minds of white people— greatly simplified the task of those among the intelligentsia who did not have to research the many behavioral differences between blacks and whites in America— or the many comparable or larger differences between other groups in other countries around the world— that have led to other intergroup complications, frictions and polarizations, which were in many cases at least as great as those between black and white Americans. Nor did intellectuals have to confront the constraints, costs and dangers inherent in group differences in behavior and values. To the intelligentsia of this later period, racial problems could be reduced to problems inside people's minds, and especially to racism, not only simplifying problems but enabling intellectuals to assume their familiar stance of being on the side of the angels against the forces of evil— and morally superior to the society in which they lived.

Life magazine, for example, greeted publication of *An American Dilemma* as showing that America was a "psychotic case among nations."[9] As with many other such sweeping pronouncements, it was not based on any empirical comparisons. For example, the number of blacks lynched in the entire history of the United States would be a fraction of the Armenians slaughtered by Turkish mobs in *one year* in the Ottoman Empire, the Ibos slaughtered by Hausa-Fulani mobs in one year in Nigeria, not to mention the number of Jews slaughtered by mobs in one year in a number of countries at various times scattered throughout history. While specifically black-white relations in the United States— especially in the South— were more polarized than black-white relations in some other countries, there were even more polarized relations between other groups that were not different in skin color in many other places and times, the Balkans and Rwanda being just two examples in our own times.

Gunnar Myrdal's basic premise— that racial problems in America were fundamentally problems inside the heads of white people, and that the resulting discrimination or neglect explained black-white differences in economic and other outcomes— was to remain the fundamental assumption of liberal thinking and policies for decades thereafter. As Professor Alfred Blumrosen of Rutgers University, an important figure in the evolution of federal racial policies, put it, discrimination should be "broadly defined," for example, by "including all conduct which adversely affects minority group employment opportunities."[10] This particular formulation preempts the very possibility that any behavior or performance by minorities themselves plays a role in the economic, educational and other "disparities" and "gaps" which are common among racial or other groups in countries around the world.

Such feats of verbal virtuosity were not peculiar to Professor Blumrosen, but were common among the intelligentsia of the liberal era. Even where there were demonstrable differences in behavior among racial or ethnic groups— whether in crime rates or rates of unwed motherhood, for example— these were more or less automatically attributed to adverse treatment, past or present, by the white majority.

Celebrated black writer James Baldwin, for example, claimed that blacks took the building of a subsidized housing project in Harlem as "additional proof of how thoroughly the white world despised them" because "people in Harlem know they are living there because white people do not think they are good enough to live anywhere else." Therefore "they had scarcely moved in" to the new housing project, before "naturally" they "began smashing windows, defacing walls, urinating in the elevators, and fornicating in the playgrounds."[11]

From this perspective, anything negative that blacks do is the fault of whites. But however much Baldwin's picture might fit the prevailing vision of the 1960s, anyone who is serious about whether it also fits the facts would have to ask such questions as: (1) Was there a time before the 1960s when it was common for blacks to urinate in public areas of buildings where they lived? and (2) If not, was that because they felt that whites had higher regard for them in earlier times?

To ask such questions is to answer them, and the answer in both cases is clearly *No!** But few asked such questions, which remained outside the sealed bubble of the prevailing vision. What was different about the 1960s was the proliferation of people like James Baldwin, promoting resentments and polarization, and making excuses for counterproductive and even barbaric behavior. Nor is this a phenomenon peculiar to blacks or even to the United States. Writing about lower-class whites in British public housing projects, Dr. Theodore Dalrymple observed: "The public spaces and elevators of all public housing blocks I know are so deeply impregnated with urine that the odor is ineradicable. And anything smashable has been smashed."[12]

The people behaving this way in Britain have none of the history that is supposed to explain black behavior in the United States. What is the same in both situations has been a steady drumbeat of grievance and victimhood ideologies from the media, from educational institutions and from other institutions permeated by the vision of the intelligentsia. In the United States, the racial version of such notions has not been confined to a fringe of

---

* As a personal note, I lived in Harlem in the 1940s and 1950s, when no one expected the smell of urine to be the norm in places where blacks lived. Others familiar with that period likewise paint a radically different picture of the projects of that era. For example: "These were not the projects of idle, stinky elevators, of gang-controlled stairwells where drug deals go down. In the 1940s, '50s and '60s, when most of the city's public housing was built, a sense of pride and community permeated well-kept corridors, apartments and grounds." Lizette Alvarez, "Out, and Up," *New York Times*, May 31, 2009, Metropolitan section p.1. The projects in which economist Walter Williams grew up in Philadelphia in that era were likewise radically different from the projects of later years. Walter E. Williams, *Up From the Projects: An Autobiography* (Stanford: Hoover Institution Press, 2010), pp. 4–8. There was certainly not less discrimination or racism in this earlier period, so the difference was not due to white people. Among the differences between the two eras was that the intelligentsia, both black and white, became more prone in the later period to make excuses such as James Baldwin made for moral squalor and barbaric behavior. After such notions permeated the society, barbaric behavior and moral squalor became accepted norms within some segments of society— and among many intellectuals observing those segments of society.

extremists. Urban League director Whitney M. Young, regarded as a racial moderate, echoed the same 1960s vision when he said, in an article in *Ebony* magazine, "most white Americans do not link the rapid spread of blight and decay of our central cities to racism. But it is the main cause." He added, "The white man creates the ghettos and brutalizes and exploits the people who inhabit them— and then he fears them and then he flees from them." The white man, according to Young, "creates a climate of despair and then acts surprised when the protest marches fill the streets and riots erupt."[13]

Jean-Paul Sartre has been credited, if that is the word, with originating the practice of excusing violence by depicting the violence of some as reactions to other things that have been analogized to violence or redefined as violence.[14] That verbal tactic has since crossed the Atlantic. After the ghetto riots of the 1960s, whose violence shocked many Americans, Professor Kenneth B. Clark, best known for his work being cited in the case of *Brown v. Board of Education*, responded by saying:

> The real danger of Harlem is not in the infrequent explosions of random lawlessness. The frightening horror of Harlem is the chronic day-to-day quiet violence to the human spirit which exists and is accepted as normal.[15]

A writer in *The Nation* magazine likewise referred to "the quiet violence in the very operation of the system." The "institutional form of quiet violence operates when people are deprived of choices in a systematic way by the very manner in which transactions normally take place."[16] A committee of black clergymen took out an ad in the *New York Times*, deploring "the silent and covert violence which white middle-class America inflicts upon the victims of the inner city."[17]

Although many of those who said such things spoke in the name of the black community, or claimed to be conveying what most blacks believed, a 1967 poll found that 68 percent of blacks said that they had more to lose than to gain from rioting.[18] After the Rodney King riots in 1992, 58 percent of blacks condemned those riots, while only 32 percent found the violence even partially justified.[19]

This, however, was not the impression created in the media, after either the earlier or the later ghetto riots. In 1967, under the headline, "The Hard-Core Ghetto Mood," *Newsweek* quoted those individuals, inside and outside the ghetto, who expressed the militant vision accepted by the intelligentsia. "Rage is common to all of them," black academician Alvin Poussaint said of ghetto blacks. A white academic in California likewise said that the Watts riots represented "the metamorphosis of the Negroes" from victims to master. "The people of Watts felt that for those four days they represented all Negroes; the historic plight of the Negroes; all the rebellions against all injustice. . . What must be understood by the rest of America is that, for the lower-class Negro, riots are not criminal, but a legitimate weapon in a morally justified civil war."[20] None of those who made such sweeping pronouncements had to offer hard evidence to have their pronouncements echoed throughout the media.

Nothing is easier than to find some individuals— in any group— who share a given writer's opinion, and to quote such individuals as if their views were typical. This approach became common in media coverage of ghetto riots. *Newsweek* magazine, for example, quoted various black youths, including one described as "*a child of Detroit's ravaged ghetto,*"[21] even though (1) the poverty rate among Detroit's black population before the riots was only half of that of blacks nationwide, (2) the homeownership rate among blacks in Detroit was the highest in the nation, and (3) the unemployment rate of blacks in Detroit was 3.4 percent— lower than that among *whites* nationwide.[22]

It was *after* the riots that Detroit became a ravaged community, and remained so for decades thereafter, as businesses withdrew, taking jobs and taxes with them. But here, as elsewhere, an idea that fit the vision did not have to meet the additional requirement of fitting the facts.

Racism and Causation

At the heart of the prevailing liberal vision of race today is the notion of "racism"— a concept with multiple, elusive and sometimes mutually contradictory meanings. Sometimes the term refers simply to any adverse opinion about any racially different group, whether a minority in a given society or a group that may be a majority in some other society. This immediately transforms any adverse judgment of any aspect of a different racial group into an indictment of whoever expressed that adverse judgment, without any need to assess the evidence or analysis behind it. In short, this approach joins the long list of arguments without arguments.

At other times, the term "racism" refers more specifically to an adverse conclusion based on a belief that the genetic endowment of a particular racial group limits their potential. Other meanings include a preference for advancing the interests of one race over another, with or without any genetic theories or even any adverse assessment of the behavior, performance or potential of the group to be disfavored. For example, an argument has been made in various countries around the world for policies preferring one group over another on the ground that the group to be discriminated against is *too* formidable for others to compete against on even terms. This argument has been made in Sri Lanka, Nigeria, Malaysia, in India's states of Assam and Andhra Pradesh, and even in early twentieth century America, where Japanese immigrants were feared on grounds that their high capability and lower standard of living would permit them to undercut the prices charged by white American farmers, workers, or commercial business owners.[23]

In other words, racism defined as a preference for one race over another need not depend upon any belief that the group to be discriminated against is inferior in performance or potential, and at various times and places has been based on the opposite belief that the group that is to be discriminated against was *too* proficient for others to compete with on equal terms, for whatever reason. As a book advocating group preferences for Malays in Malaysia put it, "Whatever the Malays could do, the Chinese could do better and more cheaply."[24] A leader in a campaign for preferential policies in India's state of Andhra Pradesh said: "Are we not entitled to jobs just because we are not as qualified?"[25] In Nigeria, an advocate of group representation policies deplored what he called "the tyranny of skills."[26]

Racism not only has varying definitions, its role in arguments by intellectuals can vary greatly from its use simply as a descriptive term to its role as a causal explanation. How one chooses to characterize adverse decisions against a particular racial group may be a matter of personal semantic preferences. But to assert a causal role is to enter the realm of evidence and verification, even if the assertion contains neither. For example, a *New York Times* editorial presented a classic example of the liberal vision of racism:

> Every index of misery continues to show that the devastating effects of racism linger on in America. Blacks make up a disproportionate number of the citizens dependent on public assistance. The unemployment rates among black males and teen-agers remain at least twice as high as among whites. The proportion of blacks dropping out of the labor force altogether has doubled over the last two decades.[27]

The bare facts cited are undoubtedly true. But two of the three facts— higher unemployment and lower labor force participation among blacks than among whites— are worse today than in earlier times. By the logic of this editorial, that would imply that there was less racism in the past, *which no one believes.*

Black labor force participation rates were higher than that of whites generations ago.[28] Black unemployment rates were lower than that of whites in 1890 and, for the last time, in 1930.[29] Black 16-year-olds and 17-year-olds had a slightly lower unemployment rate than white youngsters of the same age in 1948 and only slightly higher unemployment rates than their white peers in 1949.[30] Moreover, these unemployment rates for black teenagers were a *fraction* of what they would become in later times. These low unemployment rates existed just before the minimum wage law was amended in 1950 to catch up with the inflation of the 1940s which had, for all practical purposes, repealed the minimum wage law, since inflated wages for even unskilled labor were usually well above the minimum wage level specified when the Fair Labor Standards Act was passed in 1938.

The key role of federal minimum wage laws can be seen in the fact that black teenage unemployment, even in the recession year of 1949, was a fraction of what it would become in even prosperous later years, after the series of minimum wage escalations that began in 1950.[31]

The last year in which black unemployment was lower than white unemployment— 1930— was also the last year in which there was no federal minimum wage law. The Davis-Bacon Act of 1931 was openly advocated by some members of Congress on grounds that it would stop black construction workers from taking jobs from white construction workers by working for less than the union wages of white workers.[32] Nor was the use of minimum wage laws to deliberately price competing workers out of the labor market unique to the Davis-Bacon Act or to the United States. Similar arguments were made in Canada in the 1920s, where the object was to price Japanese immigrants out of the labor market, and in South Africa in the era of apartheid, to price non-whites out of the labor market.[33]

Any group whose labor is less in demand, whether for lack of skills or for other reasons, is disproportionately priced out of labor markets when there are minimum wage laws, which are usually established in disregard of differences in skills or experience. It has not been uncommon in Western Europe, for example, for young people to have unemployment rates above 20 percent.[34]

The point here is not to claim that pricing competitors out of the market was the motivation of all or most of the supporters of the Fair Labor Standards Act. The point is that this was its effect, regardless of the intentions. In short, the empirical evidence is far more consistent with the changing patterns of black labor force participation rates and unemployment rates over time being results of minimum wage laws than with changes in the degree of racism in American society. Indeed, these patterns over time are completely inconsistent with the fact that racism was worse in the earlier period. Only the fact that the intelligentsia tend to make racism the default setting for explaining adverse conditions among blacks enables such statements as those in the *New York Times* editorial to pass muster without the slightest demand for either evidence or analysis.

It is much the same story when racism is used as an explanation for the existence of black ghettoes. If racism is simply a characterization, there may be others who prefer different characterizations, but these are matters of subjective preferences. However, if a *causal* proposition is being advanced, then it is subject to empirical verification like other causal propositions.

When racism is offered as a *causal* explanation, as distinguished from a characterization, that makes the predispositions of whites the reason for the residential segregation of blacks, among other forms of racially disparate treatment. But seeing that as a hypothesis to be tested brings us face to face with inconvenient but inescapable facts of history. For example, most blacks were *not* residentially segregated in such cities as New York, Chicago, Detroit, Philadelphia, and Washington by the end of the nineteenth century[35]— even though they had been before and would be again in the twentieth century. Do the racial predispositions of white people just come and go unpredictably? That would be an especially strange thing for predispositions to do, even if reasoned opinions change with changing circumstances.

It is a matter of historical record that there were in fact changing circumstances preceding changing racial policies in the United States, both when these were changes for the better and when they were changes for the worse. Moreover, where the circumstances changed at different times from one place to another, racial attitudes and policies also changed correspondingly at different times.

As of the early nineteenth century, residential segregation was just one of a number of restrictions placed on free blacks in both the North and the South. However, by the last decade of the nineteenth century, such residential restrictions had eroded in Northern cities to the point where W.E.B. Du Bois could write in the 1890s of "a growing liberal spirit toward the Negro in Philadelphia," in which "the community was disposed to throw off the trammels, brush away petty hindrances and to soften the harshness of race prejudice"— leading, among other things, to blacks being able to live in white neighborhoods.[36] Nor was Philadelphia unique. There were similar developments in New York, Detroit, Washington and other Northern cities.[37] Census data show a lower rate of urban residential segregation of blacks nationwide in 1890–1910 than in later decades of the twentieth century and even as late as the 2010 census.[38]

Other restrictions had eroded as well. In Detroit, blacks who had been denied the vote in 1850 were voting in the 1880s, and in the 1890s blacks were being elected to public office by a predominantly white electorate in Michigan. The black upper class in Detroit at that time had regular social interactions with whites, and their children attended high schools and colleges with whites. In Illinois during this same era, legal restrictions on access to public accommodations for blacks were removed from the law, even though there were not enough black voters at the time to influence public policy, so that this represented changes in white public opinion.[39]

In New York City, by the 1890s most blacks did not work as unskilled laborers but held modest but respectable jobs as barbers, waiters, caterers, and skilled craftsmen. Distinguished historian Oscar Handlin characterized blacks in New York at that time as being "better off than the mass of recent white immigrants."[40] The visible improvement in the living standards of blacks was noted in Jacob Riis' 1890 classic, *How the Other Half Lives*.[41]

In Philadelphia, blacks were among the leading caterers in the city, serving a predominantly white clientele.[42] In Chicago, there were also successful black businesses serving a predominantly white clientele[43] and, as late as 1910, more than two-thirds of the city's black residents lived in neighborhoods that were predominantly white.[44]

To maintain that residential and other racial restrictions on blacks were simply a matter of the predispositions of the white population— racism— immediately raises the question of why such predispositions should have changed so much during the course of the nineteenth century— and then changed back again, drastically, and within a very few years— during the early twentieth century. But this pattern of progress in race relations in Northern urban communities during the nineteenth century, followed by retrogression in the early twentieth century, followed again by progress in the latter part of the twentieth century, is more readily understood in terms of causes other than pure subjective mood swings in the white population. In short, whether or not attitudes within the white population deserve the *characterization* of racism, a *causal* analysis of the major changes that occurred in residential and other restrictions on blacks cannot explain such *changes* by simply saying "racism."

Turning from the white population to the black population, we find developments that make the changing residential patterns explicable without resorting to inexplicable changes inside the heads of white people. Beginning at the beginning, African slaves were brought into American society at the bottom, and concentrated in the South— a region with its own cultural handicaps that produced marked differences between the *white* populations of the North and South that many observers noted during the antebellum era.[45] This meant that those blacks who came out of the South to live in Northern cities would be very different in many ways from the white populations of those cities. The visible racial differences made blacks easy to identify and restrict.

During the course of the nineteenth century, however, over a period of generations Northern blacks tended to acquire more of the culture of the surrounding white urban population of the North, just as other groups often have when living surrounded by a vastly larger population with a different culture and a higher socioeconomic level. By the end of the nineteenth century, this cultural assimilation had reached the point where racial barriers eased considerably in the Northern cities, where the black populations of these cities were now predominantly native-born residents, rather than migrants from the South.[46]

This situation changed drastically, however, and within a relatively few years, with the mass migrations of millions of blacks out of the South, beginning in the early twentieth century. This not only greatly multiplied the black populations living in many Northern cities, the newcomers were seen by both the pre-existing black populations and the white populations of these cities as creating greatly increased social problems such as crime, violence and offensive behavior in general.[47]

If these were mere "prejudices," "perceptions" or "stereotypes" in the minds of white people, as so many adverse judgments have been automatically characterized, why did the very same views appear among Northern-born blacks at the same time?

Where hard data are available, these data substantiate the pattern of behavioral differences between the pre-existing Northern black populations and the newcomers from the South. In early twentieth-century Pennsylvania, for example, the rate of violent crimes among blacks from the South was nearly five times that among blacks born in Pennsylvania.[48] In Washington, D.C., where the influx from the South occurred decades earlier, the effect of the Southerners' arrival could be seen decades earlier. For example, out of wedlock births were just under 10 percent of all births among blacks in Washington in 1878, but this more than doubled by 1881, following a large influx of Southern blacks, and remained high for years thereafter.[49]

The new majorities of Southern blacks in the Northern black urban communities were sufficiently large, and their culture sufficiently reinforced by continuing new arrivals from the South, that their rate of assimilation to the cultural norms of the surrounding white society was neither as rapid nor as complete as that of the much smaller numbers of blacks who had preceded them in these cities in the nineteenth century. Moreover, as late as 1944, Gunnar Myrdal's *An American Dilemma* pointed out that a majority of blacks living in the North at that time had been born in the South.[50]

During the early years of mass migration of blacks out of the South, many Northern-born blacks condemned the Southern newcomers, and saw in them a danger that the white population would put up new barriers against all blacks[51]— which is in fact what happened. After the massive inflow of Southern blacks into Northern cities in which small black populations had once lived scattered in predominantly white neighborhoods, these now became cities in which blacks were prevented from living in white neighborhoods by methods ranging from legal prohibitions and restrictive covenants to outright violence. All this happened within a very few years of the mass migrations of Southern blacks to Northern cities.

The massive black ghettoes which became common in the twentieth century were just one aspect of a more general retrogression in race relations, in which various public accommodations once open to blacks were now closed to them, and black children who had once gone to schools with white children in Northern cities were now segregated into different schools.[52]

The conclusion that this change was a reaction to a mass in-migration of less acculturated blacks from the South is reinforced by the history of cities on the west coast, where this mass in-migration from the South took place decades later, largely during the Second World War, and was likewise followed by retrogressions in race relations there at this later time.[53] A similar pattern had already unfolded among Jews in the United States in the late nineteenth century, when the highly acculturated German Jews lost much of the social acceptance which they had already achieved, after larger masses of much less acculturated Jews from Eastern Europe arrived, followed by new barriers against Jews in general. To say that this retrogression was caused by anti-Semitism would likewise be to transform a characterization into a causal explanation, implicitly treating those adversely affected as abstract people whose problems originated solely in other people's minds.

Whether among blacks, Jews or others, leaders within these groups themselves saw behavioral problems among some of their own people as creating backlashes in the larger society around them, from which the entire group suffered. As a result, organized social uplift groups, both secular and religious, arose within the black community, the Jewish community, as well as within other communities, aimed at changing the behavior of members of their own respective groups, in order to facilitate the advancement of these groups as a whole.[54]

Among Jews, during the era of mass immigration from Eastern Europe, the already acculturated German Jews living in America took the lead in seeking to acculturate the Jewish newcomers from Eastern Europe. A German Jewish publication of that era described the Eastern European Jews as "slovenly in dress, loud in manners, and vulgar in discourse." As a leading study of American Jews noted: "The Germans found it hard to understand what could better serve their ill-mannered cousins than rapid lessons in civics, English, and the uses of soap."[55] Such problems were not peculiar to Jews but were common among the Irish immigrants before them and to blacks after them.

During the mass migrations of blacks out of the South during the early twentieth century, both the *Chicago Defender* (a black newspaper) and the Urban League offered such published advice as:

DON'T USE VILE LANGUAGE IN PUBLIC PLACES.
DON'T THROW GARBAGE IN THE BACKYARD OR ALLEY
OR KEEP DIRTY FRONT YARDS.
DO NOT CARRY ON LOUD CONVERSATIONS IN STREET
CARS AND PUBLIC PLACES.[56]

Although these efforts produced positive results over the years, whether among blacks, Jews or others, that whole approach was antithetical to a new social philosophy that emerged in the late twentieth century— multiculturalism.

THE MULTICULTURALISM ERA

The era of multiculturalism might be considered an extension of the liberal era, but it has evolved characteristics that go not only beyond, but in some cases counter to, the characteristics of the liberal era, as that era had developed in the wake of Myrdal's *An American Dilemma* and the immediate post-World War II years. The earlier liberalism was universalistic, in that it emphasized equal treatment for all individuals, "regardless of race, color or creed," in a common phrase of that era. In some places, race was not even allowed to be recorded on job applications or various other records. The initial thrust of the civil rights movement, and of laws like the Civil Rights Act of 1964, was the extension of the same rights to all citizens, irrespective of race.

It was understood that such an extension would be especially valuable to those citizens— such as blacks and other minority group members— who had previously been denied some of those rights in one way or another. But while such policies would especially benefit particular groups, the larger implication of the civil rights movement was seen as being in effect a completion of the American Revolution, by bringing its ideals to fruition for all, the goal being aimed at being to make race irrelevant to laws and policies. Whatever the merits or demerits of this particular conception, it was one attracting a broad consensus across racial lines, among both intellectuals and the general public, and bipartisan support in Congress, where a higher percentage of Republicans than Democrats voted for the Civil Rights Act of 1964, since Congressional Democrats from the South were the main opposition.

Despite the breadth of this consensus, it was short-lived. Various segments of the population began to go in different directions for different reasons. The ghetto riots that swept across many American cities in the 1960s— the first in Los Angeles, just days after passage of the Voting Rights Act of 1965, and culminated in a wave of such riots in cities across the country after the assassination of Martin Luther King, Jr., in 1968— forfeited much sympathy for blacks among the general public. Among blacks, disappointment that the economic and social advances did not match the high expectations of the social revolution that the civil rights laws and policies were to produce, provided fertile ground for more radical elements urging more extreme actions.

The consensus on racial issues that had existed just a few years earlier was giving way to polarization over those issues, within as well as between the black population and the white population, and among intellectuals. While there was little or no support among the intelligentsia for undoing the recent civil rights advances, there were bitter disputes over the direction that racial policies were taking, as those policies moved in the direction of what can broadly be called multiculturalism.

The Multicultural Vision

Multiculturalism involves more than a simple recognition of differences in cultures among different groups. It is an insistence, *a priori,* that the effects of these differences are on net balance positive and that the particular cultures found among less fortunate groups are not to be blamed for disparities in income, education, crime rates, or family disintegration, lest observers be guilty of "blaming the victim" instead of indicting society. Given that premise, it was consistent for multiculturalists to decry educators who sought to get black youngsters to speak standard English or to force Hispanic students to speak English rather than Spanish in school. An all too typical example was an author who referred to "the white Harlem schoolmarm who carps over her students' speaking differently from herself."[57]

More generally, trying to get minority groups to acculturate to the social, linguistic and other norms of the larger society around them has been viewed negatively by multiculturalists as a form of cultural imperialism.

The key word among advocates of multiculturalism became "diversity." Sweeping claims for the benefits of demographic and cultural diversity in innumerable institutions and circumstances have prevailed without a speck of evidence being asked for or given. It is one of the purest examples of arguments without arguments, and of the force of sheer repetition, insistence and intimidation.

Among many multiculturalists, saying the word "diversity" trumps mundane concerns about empirical consequences and converts preferential treatment by race— the principle fought against so long by liberals— into "social justice" when the preferences are for those minorities currently in favor among the intelligentsia. That preferential college admissions of blacks and Hispanics may have a negative effect on the admissions of Asian Americans, not to mention whites, is something usually ignored or brushed aside. Treating races as intertemporal abstractions enables those with this vision to treat discrimination against contemporary whites as somehow offsetting discrimination against blacks in the past. For example, Professor James M. McPherson, a distinguished historian at Princeton University, made the case for affirmative action this way:

> Having benefitted in so many ways from these older forms of affirmative action that favored white males, I cannot feel censorious about the newer version that may seem to disadvantage this same category— either in faculty recruitment or student admissions. And in the area of faculty promotions, if not recruitment, white males still dominate the senior ranks in many departments of history.[58]

By reducing contemporary individuals to a verbally collectivized "category," in addition to portraying whites as an intertemporal abstraction, Professor McPherson makes discrimination against flesh-and-blood individuals palatable— or at least something that can be done with only a passing expression of "empathy" for them.[59] But affirmative action costs nothing to those individuals of his generation who presumably received the unfair advantages which are to be repaid by discrimination against younger individuals who had nothing to do with past advantages or disadvantages.

Sometimes there is an implicit assumption that any lack of skills or other qualifications among blacks today is solely a result of previous discrimination— rather than any of the innumerable other factors producing equal or greater differences among other racial or ethnic groups in other countries around the world. Sometimes this belief even became explicit, as when Justice Harry Blackmun declared in the *Weber* case in 1979 that there could be "little doubt that any lack of skill has its roots in purposeful discrimination of the past."[60] Justice William J. Brennan advanced similar reasoning in the *Bakke* case, saying that Allan Bakke, a white applicant for medical school who was passed over while blacks with lesser qualifications were admitted, "would have failed to qualify" for admission in a non-discriminatory world, being outperformed in such a hypothetical world by sufficient numbers of minority applicants, whose current failure to qualify in the existing world "was due principally to the effects of past discrimination."[61]

Given these premises, four justices in the *Bakke* case saw the Supreme Court's task as "putting minority applicants in the position they would have been in if not for the evil of racial discrimination."[62] In short, those with this vision see whites who outperform blacks— economically, educationally or otherwise— as simply unjust beneficiaries of past discrimination. Only the implicit and unsubstantiated assumption that blacks would have the same skills as others in the absence of racial discrimination gives this line of reasoning any semblance of plausibility. It is as if blacks arrived in the United States from Africa with the same skills as those of whites who arrived here from Europe. The fact that whites from different parts of Europe arrived here with very different skills from one another, as well as different cultures in general, has not been allowed to disturb this vision that proceeds as if discussing abstract people in an abstract world.

Not only have the large and numerous differences in a wide range of skills among various white ethnic groups in the United States today been utterly ignored in such arguments, so have similarly wide (or wider) differences among innumerable other groups in other countries around the world, as reflected in minorities dominating whole industries in many of these countries.

While the intelligentsia may wax surprised or indignant at the low representation of blacks among the top executive officers of major American corporations, and regard that as proof of discrimination, blacks are nevertheless better represented in such elite places than Turks were among bankers or stockbrokers in the Ottoman Empire, *which the Turks controlled*, and better represented than the Malays were in the 1960s among recipients of engineering degrees from Malaysia's universities, *which the Malays controlled*, and in which therefore no one was in any position to discriminate against them.

At various places and times, similar things could be said of the Fijians in Fiji, the Poles in Poland, the Argentines in Argentina, the Ugandans in Uganda and many other majorities grossly outperformed by their respective minorities.

While facts would undermine the hypothesis of current intergroup differentials being automatically a result of current or past discrimination, such facts have no effect on beliefs that are treated as axioms essential to a desired conclusion, rather than as hypotheses subject to verification. Those who question the prevailing vision have been accused of denying a history of racial discrimination. But, although such discrimination exists, just as cancer exists, nevertheless intergroup differences cannot be assumed *a priori* to be due to discrimination, any more than deaths can be assumed *a priori* to be due to cancer.

The premises of multiculturalism are more than an intellectual issue that might be debated around a seminar table or in academic publications. They have real world consequences affecting millions of human beings, both minorities and non-minorities, as well as the cohesion or polarization of whole societies. These consequences have been both practical and psychic, affecting economic and educational outcomes, as well as people's sense of group identity. Those who promote the preservation of racial or ethnic identities have seldom investigated what happens when lagging groups do that, compared to what happens when they follow the opposite approach. The benefits of separate cultures and identities are instead treated as axioms rather than hypotheses— in short, as arguments without arguments.

Chapter 7

Race and Cosmic Justice

The kind of collective justice demanded for racial or ethnic groups is often espoused as "social justice," but could more aptly be called *cosmic* justice, since it seeks to undo disparities created by circumstances, as well as those created by the injustices of human beings. Moreover, cosmic justice not only extends from individuals to groups, it extends beyond contemporary groups to intertemporal abstractions, of which today's groups are conceived as being the current embodiments.

DISPARITIES VERSUS INJUSTICES

Against the background of world history, the idea that an absence of an even distribution of groups in particular endeavors is something strange, or is weighty evidence of discrimination, is a dogma for which evidence is seldom asked or given— and a dogma that defies vast amounts of evidence to the contrary. Yet that dogma survives on the basis of contemporary peer consensus, even among those who take pride in considering themselves to be "thinking people." Yet this unsubstantiated presupposition of the prevailing vision is so powerful that its reverberations are felt, not only among people in the media who are ready to burst into indignation or outrage at statistical differences in outcomes among groups, but even in courts of law where employers, mortgage lenders and others whose decisions *convey* some of the differences among groups are presumed to be the *cause* of those differences— and are charged with proving their innocence, completely contrary to the practice in most other aspects of American law.

Among intellectuals who confuse blame with causation, the question-begging phrase "blaming the victim" has become a staple in discussions of intergroup differences. No individual or group can be blamed for being born into circumstances (including cultures) that lack the advantages that other people's circumstances have. But neither can "society" be automatically assumed to be either the cause or the cure for such disparities. Still less can a particular institution whose employment, pricing or lending decisions *convey* intergroup differences be automatically presumed to be *causing* those differences.

Even if one believes that environment is the key to intergroup differences, that environment includes a cultural legacy from the past— and the past is as much beyond our control as the geographic settings and historic happenstances that have left not only different individuals or races, but whole nations and civilizations, with very different heritages. Too often "environment" is conceived as the immediate surroundings today, when the cultural legacy of the past may be an equal or greater environmental influence, depending on the circumstances.

If the dogmas of multiculturalism declare different cultures equally valid, and hence sacrosanct against efforts to change them, then these dogmas simply complete the sealing off of a vision from facts— and sealing off many people in lagging groups from the advances available from other cultures around them— leaving nothing but an agenda of resentment-building and crusades on the side of the angels against the forces of evil— however futile or even counterproductive these may turn out to be for those who are the ostensible beneficiaries of such moral melodramas.

Nor can whole cultures always be left unchanged while simply tacking on new skills, since the very desire, efforts and perseverance required to acquire and master those skills are not independent of the existing culture. Moreover, the corollary of the presumed equality of cultures— that existing disparities are due to injustices inflicted by others— reduces a felt need to subject oneself to the demanding process of changing one's own capabilities, habits and outlook.

The perspective of cosmic justice is implicit in much of what is said and done by many intellectuals on many issues— for example, best-selling author Andrew Hacker's depiction of people like himself who tend "to murmur, when seeing what so many blacks endure, that there but for an accident of birth, go I."[1] However valid this may be as a general statement of the vision of cosmic justice and cosmic injustice, the word "endure" implies something more than that. It implies that the misfortunes of those on the short end of cosmic injustices are due to what they must endure at the hands of other people, rather than being due to either external circumstances that presented fewer opportunities for them to acquire valuable human capital or internal cultural values which worked against their taking advantage of the opportunities already available to them.

In this, Professor Hacker has been in the long tradition of intellectuals who more or less automatically transform differences into inequities and inequities into the evils or shortcomings of society. Among the many feats of verbal virtuosity by Andrew Hacker and others is transforming negative facts about the group that is considered to be the victim of society into mere *perceptions* by that society. Thus Professor Hacker refers to "what we call crime," to "so-called riots," and to "what we choose to call intelligence."[2] Such exercises in verbal cleansing extend to racism, from which blacks are definitionally exempt, according to Hacker, by the newly minted proviso of possessing power[3]— a proviso which serves no other purpose than providing an escape hatch from the obvious. All this clearly puts Hacker on the side of the angels, rather explicitly when he says, "On the whole, conservatives don't really care whether black Americans are happy or unhappy,"[4] as presumably liberals like himself do.

Professor Hacker expresses empathy with those blacks who work in predominantly white organizations and "are expected to think and act in white ways"[5]— the same kind of objection made by Latvians and Czechs in times past, when acquiring another culture was the price of their rising in a world where their own culture did not equip them with the same prerequisites for achievement as Germans already had. Apparently people are to think and behave as they have in the past and yet somehow get better results in the future— and, if they don't get better results, that is considered to be society's fault. Achieving the same results as others, without having to change, in order to acquire the same cultural prerequisites that others acquired without changing, would be cosmic justice, *if it happened,* but hardly a promising agenda in the real world.

Multiculturalism, like the caste system, tends to freeze people where the accident of birth has placed them. Unlike the caste system, multiculturalism holds out the prospect that, all cultures being equal, one's life chances should be the same— and that it is society's fault if these chances are not the same. Although both caste and multiculturalism suppress individual opportunities, they differ primarily in that the caste system preaches resignation to one's fate and multiculturalism preaches resentment of one's fate. Another major difference between caste and multiculturalism is that no one was likely to claim that the caste system was a boon to the lower castes.

As for more general questions about racial or ethnic identity, the costs of an identity ideology include not only the advancement that is forfeited, but also the needless disadvantages of letting people who represent the lowest common denominator of a group have a disproportionate influence on the fate of the group as a whole.

If criminals, rioters and vandals from within the group are to be automatically defended or excused for the sake of group solidarity, then the costs of that solidarity include not only a lower standard of living, since such people raise the costs of doing business in their neighborhoods and thereby raise the prices of goods and services above what they are in other neighborhoods, such people also cause fewer businesses to locate in their neighborhoods and fewer taxis to be willing to take people to such neighborhoods. Worst of all, the damage committed by those representing the lowest common denominator— encompassing crimes up to and including murder— is overwhelmingly against other members of their own group.

The high costs of putting race-based solidarity ahead of behavior and its consequences include letting the lowest common denominator become a disproportionate influence in defining the whole community itself, not only in the eyes of the larger society but also within the community. When middle-class black youngsters feel a need or pressure to adopt some of the counterproductive attitudes, values or lifestyles of the lowest common denominator, including negative attitudes toward education, lest they be accused of "acting white," then the life chances of whole generations can be sacrificed on the altar to racial solidarity. Yet a sense of the overriding importance of solidarity based on race extends far beyond children in school and goes far back in history. Gunnar Myrdal's 1944 classic, *An American Dilemma*, pointed out that it had long been the practice of black Americans to "protect any Negro from the whites, even when they happen not to like that individual Negro."[6]

When outsiders' criticisms of any segment of a community cannot be either accepted or refuted, the response is often to claim that these critics are "blaming the victim." But this whole concept confuses blame with causation. The masses of less educated and less acculturated blacks, whose migrations out of the South in the twentieth century and whose arrival in Northern cities led to retrogressions in race relations in the early part of the century— and whose later arrival in west coast cities during the Second World War led to similar retrogressions on the west coast— could hardly be blamed for having been born where they were and having absorbed the culture which existed around them in the South. But that does not deny these migrants' causal role in the changes for the worse which occurred in cities outside the South after the Southern blacks' arrivals there.

No one in John Rawls' "original position" as a disembodied being contemplating alternative circumstances into which to be born would have chosen to be born black in the South of that era. From a cosmic perspective, it was an injustice to those who were. But that is very different from saying that their mass migrations in search of a better life did not impose large costs on both the black and white populations already residing in the Northern cities to which they moved, or that these latter had no right to resent these costs or to try to protect themselves from them. The inherent conflict of these different legitimate desires and interests in each of these groups is part of the tragedy of the human condition— as contrasted with a simple moral melodrama starring the intelligentsia on the side of the angels against the forces of evil.

RACE AND CRIME

The intelligentsia's feats of verbal virtuosity reach their heights— or depths— when discussing the crime rate among blacks in America. For example, *New York Times* columnist Tom Wicker responded to an incident in which a white woman jogging in Central Park was gang raped by black youths, by denying that this was a racially motivated crime. Wicker said, "the fact that the victim was white and the attackers black does not seem to have caused the crime." He added:

> But if race does not explain this crime, race was relevant to it. The attackers lived surrounded and surely influenced by the social pathologies of the inner city. They hardly could have reached teen age without realizing and resenting the wide economic and social gap that still separates blacks and whites in this country; and they could not fail to see, and probably return, the hostility that glares at them undisguised across that gap. These influences are bound to have had some consequences— perhaps long repressed, probably not realized or understood— in their attitudes and behavior.[7]

The "wide economic and social gap" between blacks and whites that Wicker referred to was even wider in earlier years, when it was common for whites to go up to Harlem at night for public entertainment or private parties, and common for both blacks and whites to sleep out in the city's parks on hot summer nights during an era when most people could not afford air-conditioning. But sleeping in parks— or in some cases, even walking through some of those same parks in broad daylight— became dangerous in later and more prosperous times. Yet here, as elsewhere, the prevailing vision often seems impervious to even the plainest facts.

The role played by many people who, like Tom Wicker himself, have incessantly emphasized "gaps" and "disparities" as injustices to be resented, rather than lags to be overcome, is seldom considered to be among the candidates for inclusion among the "root causes" of crime, even though the rise of crime is far more consistent with the increasing prevalence of such grievance and resentment ideologies than with other things that are considered to be "root causes," such as poverty levels, which have been declining as crime rates rose. Resentments, based on ideologies of cosmic justice, are not confined to the intelligentsia but "trickle down" to others. For example, right after charges of gang rape of a black woman were filed against white students on Duke University's lacrosse team in 2006, angry reactions from a black college in the same town reflected that same vision, as reported in *Newsweek*:

Across town, at NCCU, the mostly black college where the alleged victim is enrolled, students seemed bitterly resigned to the players' beating the rap. "This is a race issue," said Candice Shaw, 20. "People at Duke have a lot of money on their side." Chan Hall, 22, said, "It's the same old story. Duke up, Central down." Hall said he wanted to see the Duke students prosecuted "whether it happened or not. It would be justice for things that happened in the past."[8]

Implicit in these statements are the key elements of the cosmic justice vision of the intelligentsia— seeing other people's good fortune as a grievance, rather than an incentive for self-improvement, and seeing flesh-and-blood contemporaries as simply part of an intertemporal abstraction, so that a current injustice against them would merely offset other injustices of the past. There could hardly be a more deadly inspiration for a never-ending cycle of revenge and counter-revenge— the Hatfields and the McCoys writ large, with a whole society caught in the crossfire.

The built-in excuse has become as standard in discussions of black crime as it is unsubstantiated, except by peer consensus among the intelligentsia. The phrase "troubled youth" is a common example of the unsubstantiated but built-in excuse, since those who use that phrase usually feel no need to offer any specific evidence about the specific individuals they are talking about, who may be creating big trouble for others, while enjoying themselves in doing so. An all too common pattern across the country was that in an episode in Milwaukee:

Shaina Perry remembers the punch to her face, blood streaming from a cut over her eye, her backpack with her asthma inhaler, debit card and cellphone stolen, and then the laughter. . . "They just said, 'Oh, white girl bleeds a lot,'" said Perry, 22, who was attacked at Kilbourn Reservoir Park over the Fourth of July weekend. . . Milwaukee Police Chief Edward Flynn noted Tuesday that crime is colorblind... "I saw some of my friends on the ground getting beat pretty severely.". . . Perry needed three stitches to close a cut above her eye. She said she saw a friend getting kicked and when she walked up to ask what was happening, a man punched her in the face. "I heard laughing as they were beating everybody up. They were eating chips like it was a picnic," said Perry, a restaurant cashier. . . Most of the 11 people who told the Journal Sentinel they were attacked or witnessed the attacks on their friends said that police did not take their complaints seriously. . . "About 20 of us stayed to give statements and make sure everyone was accounted for. The police wouldn't listen to us, they wouldn't take our names or statements. They told us to leave. It was completely infuriating."[9]

Variations on such episodes of unprovoked violence by young black gangs against white people on beaches, in shopping malls or in other public places have occurred in Philadelphia, New York, Denver, Chicago, Cleveland, Washington, Los Angeles and other places across the country, often with the attackers voicing anti-white invective and mocking those they left injured or bleeding.[10] But such episodes are often either ignored or downplayed in most of the media, and by officials— and the *Chicago Tribune* even offered an excuse for not reporting the race of the attackers in a series of such episodes that alarmed the Chicago public.[11] Yet race is widely reported when it comes to imprisonment rates or other racial disparities. For example:

> In March of 2010, Secretary of Education Arne Duncan delivered a speech that highlighted racial disparities in school suspension and expulsion and that called for more rigorous civil rights enforcement in education. He suggested that students with disabilities and Black students, especially males, were suspended far more often than their White counterparts. These students, he also noted, were often punished more severely for similar misdeeds. Just months later, in September of 2010, a report analyzing 2006 data collected by the U.S. Department of Education's Office for Civil Rights found that more than 28% of Black male middle school students had been suspended at least once. This is nearly three times the 10% rate for white males. Further, 18% of Black females in middle school were suspended, more than four times as often as white females (4%). Later that same month, U.S. Attorney General Eric Holder and Secretary Duncan each addressed a conference of civil rights lawyers in Washington, D.C., and affirmed their departments' commitment to ending such disparities.[12]

The very possibility that there might be behavioral differences behind the punishment differences does not surface in such discussions. To believe that there are no behavioral differences between black and white school-age males is to assume that the large and undeniable differences in crime rates— including murder rates— between black and white young adults suddenly and inexplicably materialize after they finish school.

Professor David D. Cole of the Georgetown University Law School expressed views similar to those of Tom Wicker and many others among the intelligentsia of the multicultural era, when he lamented the increasing imprisonment of black men:

> In the 1950s, when segregation was still legal, African-Americans comprised 30 percent of the prison population. Sixty years later, African-Americans and Latinos make up 70 percent of the incarcerated population, and that population has skyrocketed. The disparities are greatest where race and class intersect— nearly 60 percent of all young black men born between 1965 and 1969 who dropped out of high school went to prison at least once on a felony conviction before they turned thirty-five.[13]

Professor Cole posed the issue explicitly in the cosmic justice terms of John Rawls:

> Were we in John Rawls' "original position," with no idea whether we would be born a black male in an impoverished urban home. . . would we accept a system in which one out of every three black males born today can expect to spend time in jail during his life.[14]

The preemptive assertion in passing that it is the *system*— something external, created by others in the larger society— that is the cause of the problem arbitrarily puts off limits at the outset the very possibility that the problem may be elsewhere. By sheer verbal virtuosity, rather than by any facts or evidence, collective responsibility is put on those in the larger society. There is clearly *something* in the circumstances into which many black males are born that makes it far more likely that they will commit crimes than is true of the population in general, including the majority of the black population that does *not* end up behind bars. But that tells us absolutely nothing about what that something is. If it is being "impoverished," then clearly there is a lot less poverty today than in 1950, when the imprisonment rate among black males was lower, even though invoking poverty remains at least as much a part of the rituals— as distinguished from arguments— of intellectuals today as then.

Professor Cole adds some other statistics, that "only 5 percent of college-educated African-Americans" have spent time in prison, while the imprisonment rate for black male high-school dropouts "is nearly fifty times the national average."[15] He also notes, "Children with parents in prison are in turn seven times more likely to be imprisoned at some point in their lives than other children."[16] None of this supports the claim that the cause is an external "system," as asserted by Professor Cole, rather than an internal counterproductive culture, perhaps aided and abetted by outsiders who excuse or even celebrate that counterproductive underclass culture— an underclass culture which has produced very similar results among lower class whites in Britain,[17] where similar ideologies of envy and resentment have long been promoted by the British intelligentsia.

Both in Britain and in the United States, as well as in other countries, there has been a steady ideological drumbeat of rhetoric from intellectuals depicting "gaps" and "disparities" as grievances against those who are better off. In both Britain and America, this resentment and hostility generated by the intelligentsia has been directed by those who accept it, not only against members of the larger society, but also against those members of their own group who are working to do well in school, in order to have a better life later on.

What is truly remarkable in its implications is the contrast between the higher rate of imprisonment among young men in the black ghettos of America today compared to the 1950s, and how that undermines the very argument in which these imprisonment rates are cited. Surely the supposed "root causes" of crime— poverty, discrimination and the like— were not *less* in the 1950s, before the civil rights laws and policies of the 1960s. And what of those blacks who do *not* drop out of high school but who go on to college instead— and seldom end up in prison? It should also be noted that, from 1994 on into the twenty-first century, the poverty rate among black husband-wife families was below 10 percent.[18] Are these blacks living in a different external "system" or do they have a different internal culture, representing different values in their families or among others who have influenced them?

Yet such questions are seldom asked, much less answered. Instead, today's higher rate of incarceration is blamed on drug laws, tighter sentencing rules, and a general failure of society. In short, society is to blame, except apparently for those members of society who actually commit the crimes. But, whatever the reasons for the higher crime rate now than then, or between blacks and whites, it is indeed a tragic injustice— *from a cosmic perspective*— to be born into circumstances that make it more likely that one will commit crimes and be imprisoned, with negative consequences for the rest of one's life. If some personified Fate had decreed this, then that would be the perpetrator of the injustice. But, if this is just part of the way the world has evolved, then it is a cosmic injustice— if something as impersonal as the cosmos can be considered capable of being unjust.

As noted in Chapter 4, a *cosmic* injustice is not a *social* injustice, and proceeding as if society has both the omniscience and the omnipotence to "solve" the "problem" risks *anti-social* justice, in which others are jeopardized or sacrificed, in hopes of putting some particular segment of the population where they would be "but for" being born into adverse circumstances that they did not choose. It is certainly no benefit to blacks in general to take a sympathetic view of those blacks who commit crimes, since most of the crimes committed by blacks— especially murder— are committed against other blacks.

Whatever the injustices of society that might be blamed as "root causes" of crime, the black victims of crime are not responsible for those injustices. Here, especially, "social justice" in theory becomes *anti-social* justice in practice, sacrificing innocent people's well-being— or even their lives— because some other individuals are considered not to have been born into circumstances that would have given them as good a chance as others have had to achieve their own well-being without becoming criminals. Moreover, it is wholly arbitrary to imagine oneself in Rawls' "original position" as a potential black criminal, rather than as one of the far more numerous blacks who are victims of criminals.

Those who say that we should "do something" seldom face the fact that everything depends on just what specifically that something is. Being lenient with criminals has not worked. Relieving poverty has not reduced crime. And certainly being "non-judgmental" has not done so either. Crime rates skyrocketed when all these things were tried, whether among blacks or whites, and whether in America or in England.

The automatic "celebration" of cultural differences, or the non-judgmental view of socially counterproductive behavior, for example, cannot be continued if the goal is to improve the well-being of actual flesh-and-blood people, rather than seeking cosmic justice for an intertemporal abstraction. One can be humane or inhumane only to living people, not to abstractions.

SLAVERY

Nowhere have intellectuals seen racial issues as issues about intertemporal abstractions more so than in discussions of slavery. Moreover, few facts of history have been so distorted by highly selective filtering as has the history of slavery. To many people today, slavery means white people holding black people in bondage. The vast millions of people around the world who were neither white nor black, but who were either slaves or enslavers for centuries, fade out of this vision of slavery, as if they had never existed, even though they may well have outnumbered both blacks and whites. It has been estimated that there were more slaves in India than in the entire Western Hemisphere.[19] China during the era of slavery has been described as "one of the largest and most comprehensive markets for the exchange of human beings in the world."[20] Slaves were a majority of the population in some of the cities in Southeast Asia.[21] At some period or other in history, as John Stuart Mill pointed out, "almost every people, now civilized, have consisted, in majority, of slaves."[22]

When Abraham Lincoln said, "If slavery is not wrong, nothing is wrong,"[23] he was expressing an idea peculiar to Western civilization at that time, and by no means universally accepted throughout Western civilization. What seems almost incomprehensible today is that there was no serious challenge to the moral legitimacy of slavery prior to the eighteenth century. Christian monasteries in Europe and Buddhist monasteries in Asia both had slaves. Even Thomas More's fictional ideal society, Utopia, had slaves.

Although intellectuals today may condemn slavery as a historic evil of "our society," what was peculiar about Western society was not that it had slaves, like other societies around the world, but that it was the first civilization to turn *against* slavery— and that it spent more than a century destroying slavery, not only within Western civilization itself, but also in other countries around the world, over the often bitter and sometimes armed resistance of people in other societies. Only the overwhelming military power of Western nations during the age of imperialism made this possible. Slavery did not quietly die out of its own accord. It went down fighting to the bitter end, in countries around the world, and it has still not totally died out to this day, in parts of the Middle East and Africa.[24]

It is the image of *racial* slavery— white people enslaving black people— that has been indelibly burned into the consciousness of both black and white Americans today by the intelligentsia— and not simply as a fact about the past but as a *causal* factor used to explain much of the present, and an enduring *moral* condemnation of the enslaving race. Yet two crucial facts have been filtered out of this picture: (1) the institution of slavery was not based on race and (2) whites as well as blacks were enslaved. The very word "slave" is derived from the name of a European people— Slavs— who were enslaved for centuries before the first African was brought in bondage to the Western Hemisphere. It was not only in English that the word for slave derived from the word for Slav; the same was true in various other European languages and in Arabic.[25]

For most of the history of slavery, which covers most of the history of the human race, most slaves were not racially different from those who enslaved them. Not only did Europeans enslave other Europeans, Asians enslaved other Asians, Africans enslaved other Africans, Polynesians enslaved other Polynesians and the indigenous peoples of the Western Hemisphere enslaved other indigenous peoples of the Western Hemisphere.

Moreover, after it became both technologically and economically feasible to transport masses of slaves from one continent to another— that is, to have a whole population of slaves of a different race— Europeans as well as Africans were enslaved and transported from their native lands to bondage on another continent. Pirates alone transported a million or more Europeans as slaves to the Barbary Coast of North Africa— at least twice as many European slaves as there were African slaves transported to the United States and to the thirteen colonies from which it was formed.[26] Moreover, white slaves were still being bought and sold in the Islamic world, decades after blacks had been freed in the United States.

What marked the modern era of slavery in the West was the fact that, as distinguished historian Daniel Boorstin pointed out, "Now for the first time in Western history, the status of slave coincided with a difference of race."[27] But to claim that race or racism was the basis of slavery is to cite as a cause something that happened thousands of years after its supposed effect. As for the legacy of slavery in the world of today, that is something well worth investigating— as distinguished from simply making sweeping assumptions. Too many assumptions that have been made about the effects of slavery on both blacks and whites will not stand up under scrutiny.

Back during the era of slavery in the United States, such prominent writers as the French visitor and observer Alexis de Tocqueville, Northern traveler in the antebellum South Frederick Law Olmsted and prominent Southern writer Hinton Helper all pointed to striking differences between the North and the South, and attributed the deficiencies of the Southern region to the effects of slavery on the *white* population of the South.[28] These differences between Northern and Southern whites were not mere "perceptions" or "stereotypes." They were factually demonstrable in areas ranging from literacy rates to rates of unwed motherhood, as well as in attitudes toward work and violence. But attributing these differences to slavery ignored the fact that the ancestors of white Southerners differed in these same ways from the ancestors of white Northerners, when they both lived in different parts of Britain, and when neither had ever seen a black slave.[29]

Does the moral enormity of slavery give it any more decisive *causal* weight in explaining the situation of blacks today than it did in explaining that of whites in the antebellum South? There is no *a priori* answer to that question, which must be examined empirically, like many other questions.

The fact that so many black families today consist of women with fatherless children has been said by many to be a legacy of slavery. Yet most black children grew up in two-parent families, even under slavery itself, and for generations thereafter.[30] As recently as 1960, two-thirds of black children were still living in two-parent families.[31] A century ago, a slightly higher percentage of blacks were married than were whites.[32] In some years, a slightly higher percentage of blacks were in the labor force than were whites.[33] The reasons for changes for the worse in these and other patterns must be sought in our own times. Whatever the reasons for the disintegration of the black family, it escalated to the current disastrous level well over a century after the end of slavery, though less than a generation after a large expansion of the welfare state and its accompanying non-judgmental ideology.

To say that slavery will not bear the full weight of responsibility for all subsequent social problems among black Americans is not to say that it had negligible consequences among either blacks or whites, or that its consequences ended when slavery itself ended. But this is only to say that answers to questions about either slavery or race must be sought in facts, not in assumptions or visions, and certainly not in attempts to reduce questions of causation to only those which provide moral melodramas and an opportunity for the intelligentsia to be on the side of the angels.

Just as Western Europeans in post-Roman times benefitted from the fact that their ancestors had been conquered by the Romans, with all the brutality and oppression that entailed, blacks in America today have a far higher standard of living than most Africans in Africa as a result of their ancestors being enslaved, with all the injustices and abuses that entailed. There is no question that both conquest and enslavement were traumatic experiences for those on whom they were inflicted. Nor is either morally justified by whatever benefits might come of this to subsequent generations of their offspring. But history cannot be undone. Nor does conceiving of races as intertemporal abstractions have any such track record as to make it look like a promising approach to the present or the future.

Chapter 8

The Past and the Future

Wat are the implications of the many facts, beliefs and controversies about race that we have explored?

One fact that seems both blatant and inescapable is that social groups, whether racial or otherwise, have major differences in their outcomes, whether in educational institutions, in the economy or in other aspects of life. When the many factors that can influence group outcomes are considered— including geography, history, demographics, culture, happenstances and the other groups with whom they compete, whether in the market, in the schools, at the polls or on the battlefields— the probability that all these factors, and more, would work out in such a way as to produce the same end results for different groups shrinks to the vanishing point.

Yet many leading twentieth century intellectuals tended to focus on one supposedly overwhelming factor behind these intergroup differences, whether genes in the early years of that century or discrimination in the later years. Why intellectuals would do this is a fascinating, but less consequential, question than what the results of such thinking have been in the past and are likely to be in the future.

The consequences of genetic determinism have ranged from laws against racial intermarriage to eugenics to genocide. In our own times, an opposite presumption is that statistical differences in outcomes between groups imply discrimination— a presumption prevailing from the level of street corner demagogues to the august chambers of the Supreme Court of the United States. However different current presumptions are from those of the past, the same intolerance prevails toward those who think otherwise as in the earlier era of genetic determinism. This is more than a coincidental footnote

122

to intellectual history. Such dogmatism means that a whole society can paint itself into a corner when it comes to thinking about racial problems that have shown their potential to become explosive, both in the history of this country and in the history of other countries around the world.

Whole cities, of which Detroit is a classic example, have been devastated physically, economically and socially by racial problems which simply cannot be discussed honestly by any elected official who wants to remain in office or by anyone in academia or the media who does not want to become a pariah. The price of this moral paralysis is paid in blood, mostly the blood of black people victimized by black criminals, though there is some democratization of degeneration, as mobs of young black thugs have in recent years launched violent attacks on whites in shopping malls, on beaches and in other public places in cities across the United States.

Any use of force by the police, sufficient to stop these attacks, would be called "excessive" in the media and by politicians or "community leaders." The path of least resistance, in the current climate of opinion, is for the authorities and the media to ignore or downplay these attacks or— where they are too widely known locally to go unreported— to refer to them as simply unspecified "young people" attacking unspecified victims for unspecified reasons. This is done even when the attackers loudly voice their hatred of white people, who have been widely depicted to them as the source of their problems and frustrations by politicians, the media and even educational institutions from the schools to the universities— all of whom say what is politically correct to say, in the corner into which they have painted themselves.

Yet, in a sense, these racial problems are not ultimately racial. Remarkably similar degenerate acts plague Britain's white lower class, as reported in such books as *Life at the Bottom* by British physician Theodore Dalrymple. What is similar on both sides of the Atlantic is a social vision that excuses barbarism by blaming society, thus allowing the intelligentsia to align themselves on the side of the angels against the forces of evil. Here too the price of these self-indulgences is often paid in blood by those who do not have the luxury of theorizing from afar.

THE FALSE DICHOTOMY

Genetic determinism and discrimination are not just alternative hypotheses; together they create a false dichotomy with its own weighty consequences. Members of lagging groups who take this dichotomy seriously must either confess to being inherently and irretrievably inferior or else blame others for their lags. Members of more fortunate groups are left with a choice between arrogance and guilt, when confronted with the false dichotomy. History records the painful consequences of both such choices. While genetic determinism and discrimination have been presented as contrasting or even mutually exclusive or jointly exhaustive beliefs, they are in a sense mutually reinforcing— in the sense that the false dichotomy they represent paints people into a corner from which there is no apparent escape.

Members of lagging groups, especially, face extreme choices. Within the terms of the false dichotomy, they must either admit that they, their loved ones and their whole race are inherently and incurably inferior for all eternity, or else they must see outsiders as implacable enemies responsible for unconscionably inflicting needless problems and suffering on them. People who might not have reached this latter conclusion in isolation, may not only seize that conclusion but hold on to it tenaciously, in defiance of all evidence to the contrary, when they see no apparent alternative except one that is intolerable. Thus even otherwise reasonable people may succumb to racial paranoia.

Even those who can manage to escape the false dichotomy, and its intolerable alternatives, would need to recognize that those who lag, for whatever reasons, face a daunting task of bringing themselves up to the level of the rest of society in knowledge, skills, and experience— and in the attitudes necessary to acquire this knowledge and these skills and experience. Particular individuals may be able to do so within their own lifetimes, but for millions of people from a lagging group to do so would be harder and take far longer, even if their leaders were urging them in that direction, and virtually impossible when their leaders are fiercely promoting the idea that their lags are due primarily— if not solely— to the malice of other people.

The magnitude of the task, even without these ideological complications, may be suggested by considering how many centuries it took for Europe to catch up to China, technologically, intellectually and otherwise, or how many centuries Eastern Europe has lagged economically behind Western Europe, and still lags today, with a wider gap in per capita income between people in these two halves of Europe than the per capita income gap between black and white Americans. Whether within countries or between countries, the "gaps," "disparities" and "inequities" that so preoccupy intellectuals are unlikely to disappear quickly, even under ideal conditions, especially when those who are more advanced keep advancing, while those who lag can continue to lag, relatively speaking, even when they are advancing as well.

Intellectuals who made genetic determinism the overriding explanation of intergroup differences in outcomes in the early twentieth century, and discrimination the overriding explanation of these differences in the latter part of the twentieth century, have in both cases made the prevailing belief of the day obligatory for anyone who wanted to be taken seriously, or even to avoid being stigmatized as a shallow "sentimentalist" in the early part of the century, or a despised "racist" in the latter part. In both eras, intellectuals claimed the moral high ground, as saviors of their race during the era of genetic determinism and as moral crusaders against racial injustice in the era of the prevalence of discrimination theories. Nor were the intelligentsia in either era much open to other explanations of intergroup differences, which could undermine or devastate their flattering vision of themselves.

Cultural explanations of intergroup differences not only pose a threat to intellectuals' self-flattering visions, such explanations also impose a heavy burden of work, since culture is an omnibus category with numerous geographic, demographic, historical and other factors requiring large and onerous investments of time to understand, as contrasted with the ease and self-satisfaction of saying such sweeping things as "race is everything" (as Madison Grant did[1]) or that the social problem of race in America is basically "a white man's problem" caused by "confused and contradictory attitudes" in the minds of the majority population (as Gunnar Myrdal did[2]).

PROGRESS AND RETROGRESSION

There have been many examples of progress in race relations, and especially of economic progress by groups that used to lag further behind others than they do today. Many individuals and organizations have claimed credit for that progress but, as has been said in other contexts, "victory has 100 fathers and defeat is an orphan."

Those who celebrate the rise in incomes, occupations, education and in other ways among blacks, Hispanics and other American minorities— and in many cases celebrate the ideas, policies and leaders supposedly responsible for this progress— seldom even attempt to cite ideas, policies or leaders responsible for such things as a rising murder rate among blacks and others in the 1960s, despite the fact that their murder rates had been going down, especially among black males, prior to the 1960s.[3] The catastrophic decline of the black family, and the social consequences of increasing majorities of fatherless children, in the wake of the burgeoning welfare state in the 1960s, has few contemporaries prepared to take responsibility and many prepared to blame it on a "legacy of slavery," when in fact more black children grew up with two parents even under slavery, and in the generations that followed, than today.

Nor is such degeneration peculiar to the United States. In Britain, Dr. Theodore Dalrymple paints a very similar picture of a violent and disorganized subculture with family disintegration and widespread ignorance in lower-class white neighborhoods. He says of his young patients: "Very few of the sixteen-year-olds whom I meet as patients can read and write with facility; they do not even regard my question as to whether they can read and write as in the least surprising or insulting." He adds: "One can tell merely by the way these youths handle a pen or a book that they are unfamiliar with these instruments." As for mathematics: "I cannot recall meeting a sixteen-year-old white from the public housing estates that are near my hospital who could multiply nine by seven (I do not exaggerate). Even three by seven often defeats them."[4]

When a race of people who produced Shakespeare and Sir Isaac Newton now produces large numbers of young people who are functionally illiterate and unable to do simple arithmetic, do we need to resort to either genes or discrimination to explain this degeneration?

These British youths have no "legacy of slavery" to fall back on as excuses. Nor is it clear that such excuses are valid for black youths with the same behavior patterns on the other side of the Atlantic. Such behavior patterns escalated on both sides of the Atlantic with the ascendancy of the welfare state ideology that is essential to establishing a welfare state in a democratic society. Once brought into being, a welfare state can subsidize counterproductive behavior, which the welfare state ideology excuses or promotes, but which would be unsustainable without being underwritten by the taxpayers' money.

Much of the social progress among lagging groups which took place in the latter half of the twentieth century, and for which many intellectuals, politicians and others have taken credit, represents the continuation of strong trends that antedate the social legislation which has so often been regarded as the primary cause. The largest rise out of poverty among black Americans, for example, occurred *prior* to the civil rights legislation and escalating social welfare legislation of the 1960s.[5] Nor has this pattern been confined to America. Group preferences have been demanded and instituted in various parts of Europe and Asia *after* there had been a significant increase in the number of members of lagging groups who became more educated,[6] so it is difficult to disentangle how much of the group's advancement has been due to the preferences and how much is due to the rising level of education that preceded the preferences.

Where there has been a degeneration in behavior, however— whether in falling test scores or rising crime rates or other indicators— this has seldom been correlated with the kinds of factors that have been widely used as explanations, such as poverty or discrimination. Some of the most visible and most persistent degeneration, such as skyrocketing crime rates in the 1960s, occurred when poverty and discrimination were becoming demonstrably less severe.

Such external explanations do not square with the facts. Something has been happening within the minds of people, whether spontaneously or as a result of ideas spread by others. In the United States, much of this moral or ideological source of social degeneration can be traced to what can be called the race industry.

THE RACE INDUSTRY

Race is more than a biological category or a social category. It has become an industry, with its own infrastructure, branches, incentives and agendas. The most obvious examples are the political representatives of particular racial or ethnic groups, as exemplified by the Congressional Black Caucus or the Hispanic Caucus or such non-governmental organizations as La Raza or the NAACP. Many academic institutions have various ethnic studies departments or programs, and their thrust is by no means confined to academic scholarship seeking objective facts about those groups. The legal profession is also well represented among those specializing in racial issues, and here too the disinterested search for truth is seldom the overriding consideration. "Diversity" consultants in private industry and community organizers in racial or ethnic neighborhoods are among the many other occupations that are part of the race industry.

Despite the wide variety of occupations in the race industry, there are commonalities in their underlying visions and agendas. Central to their mission is the presumption that economic lags, educational deficiencies or even high crime rates among the respective groups they represent are due to the failings or malice of others. Views or facts to the contrary are to be discountenanced, or if possible banned or punished, rather than engaged.

In addition to the particular portrayal of racial or ethnic issues promoted by the race industry, there is a highly selective view of what sorts of "solutions" are needed— almost invariably these are policies or actions that enhance the role, power, prestige and economic flourishing of the race industry itself, *even if these policies or actions are demonstrably counterproductive in their effects on the people in whose name the race industry speaks.*

A classic example is the policy of preferentially admitting members of specifically selected minorities* to colleges and universities under the rubric of "affirmative action" or "diversity."

In addition to promoting particular policies, such as affirmative action, the race industry promotes more general ideas and concepts, such as "social

---

* Which do not include Asian Americans or Jewish Americans, for example.

justice" and "disparate impact." Both the specific policies and the general concepts need closer scrutiny than they usually get from the media or even academia. Since "social justice" has already been covered in Chapter 7, we can take "affirmative action" as an example of a policy, and "disparate impact" as an example of a concept, both heavily promoted by the race industry.

"Affirmative Action"

Group preference policies known as "affirmative action" in the United States have existed in many other countries around the world, often longer than they have in the United States, and under a variety of names, such as "positive discrimination" in India and Britain, "sons of the soil" preferences in Malaysia and Indonesia, and "reflecting the federal character of the country" in Nigeria.

Though based on a variety of rationales peculiar to particular countries, these group preference policies have had a remarkable similarity in their actual consequences, which have often differed considerably from the visions or rationales on which they were based.[7]

One of the common characteristics of group preference programs in many countries has been that their proponents have said that these are "temporary" programs, and in some countries there have even been specific cutoff dates for the ending of these programs. Yet these programs have been extended as these cutoff dates approached, and sometimes re-extended, but seldom, if ever, actually ended. More commonly, these programs have expanded over time, spreading to more institutions, to more processes within institutions, or to more groups.

In the United States, for example, "affirmative action" referred initially to positive steps to ensure equal opportunity "without regard to their race, creed, color or national origin." But, within a very few years, "affirmative action" took on the meaning of numerical "goals" that amounted to group quotas. In Malaysia and India, preferences spread to the grades of students that were adjusted for the benefit of groups preferentially admitted to universities.[8] In short, the expansion of preferences has been the rule, not the exception.

What might seem to be the simplest and easiest of the goals to achieve by group preferences— the advancement of the group or groups selected as beneficiaries— has in fact proved to be one of the most elusive. Although the rationale for providing preferential treatment for particular groups has usually been to aid their rise from a disadvantaged position, the actual beneficiaries of group preferences have often been individuals who have been more fortunate than other members of their group, and even more fortunate than the average member of the society as a whole. That has been true in India, in Malaysia and in the United States, among other places.

Under the headline, "With Affirmative Action, India's Rich Gain School Slots Meant for Poor," the *New York Times* reported that in that country's universities "those given set-asides at their institutions were generally the children of doctors, lawyers and high-level bureaucrats."[9] In Malaysia, just over half of the scholarships awarded under affirmative action went to Malay students whose families were in the top 17 percent of the income distribution.[10] A 2004 study found that a majority of the black alumni of Harvard were either West Indian or African immigrants, or the children of these immigrants, *not* native-born American blacks who provide the rationale for preferential admissions. Similar findings have appeared in studies of some other elite colleges.[11]

Where students from genuinely disadvantaged minority groups have been preferentially admitted to college and universities, it has been by no means certain that this has been, on net balance, a benefit, and actual harm inflicted on the supposed beneficiaries has been by no means unknown. As noted in Chapter 5, black and other minority students with the qualifications for success have been artificially turned into failures by being mismatched with academic institutions they do not qualify for under the standards applied to other students. This mismatching effect can be seen by what happened when racial preferences were banned in the University of California system.

Despite dire predictions that there would be a drastic reduction in the number of minority students in the University of California system after racial preferences in admission were banned, an empirical study showed that there were "modest declines in black and Hispanic enrollment but an increase in black and Hispanic degrees."[12] There were major declines in minority enrollment at the top-ranked Berkeley and UCLA campuses— 42 percent and 33 percent, respectively— but these declines were almost completely offset by increases in the number of minority students at the other campuses.[13] More important, there was an *increase* in the number of black and Hispanic students *graduating* from the University of California system, including an increase of 55 percent in the number graduating in four years and an increase of 63 percent in the number graduating in four years with a grade point average of 3.5 or higher. The number of black and Hispanic students who graduated with degrees in science, technology, mathematics and engineering rose by 51 percent and the number of doctorates earned by black and Hispanic students in the system rose by 25 percent after preferential admissions policies were banned.[14]

Data from other colleges and universities likewise show higher graduation rates for black students at colleges and universities when their academic qualifications are more similar to those of the other students at those institutions.[15] Moreover, black students who are mismatched with law schools do not pass the bar examination as often as black students with very similar academic qualifications who went to law schools where the other students had similar academic qualifications. The end result can be fewer black lawyers than if there were no affirmative action.[16]

The negative effects of affirmative action on the non-preferred groups, such as whites and Asian Americans, have been obvious. But when there are also negative effects on groups preferentially admitted, it is by no means clear who has gained, other than the race industry, which can trumpet the successful imposition of its agenda, ignoring the needless failures of minority students created by that agenda.

"Disparate Impact"

The indisputable fact that life has never been fair, in the sense of offering equal likelihoods of success to all, at any time or in any place, in the thousands of years of recorded history, provides an inexhaustible supply of grievances for all sorts of groups at all sorts of places and times. The question is whether we allow that to be an automatic indictment of any particular institution or any particular society for causing disparities in outcomes that are found in that particular institution or that particular society. There is no question that someone born in a slum in Brazil or Bangladesh has far less chance in life than someone born in an upscale American community. Indeed, there is no question that Americans born in different economic circumstances— or even in the same economic circumstances, but raised by families with different values— have very different chances in life.

Against this background, it is hardly surprising that different individuals and groups meet the standards in numerous kinds of endeavors to very different extents. Yet the "disparate impact" of particular standards on the success rates of different groups is widely taken as a sign of "unfairness" in the criteria themselves, rather than being a consequence of existing differences in real and relevant qualifications, which may in some instances be due to prior unfairness in the circumstances in which less qualified people were raised— or in other cases reflecting differences due to the attitudes, behavior and performances of those people themselves.

The distinction is fundamental between saying that statistical disparities found at a particular institution are *caused* by that institution, rather than saying that these disparities *convey* disparities that originate outside that institution. For example, there has been much consternation over the fact that "the poor pay more" in stores located in low-income minority neighborhoods, where stores often charge higher prices than stores located in middle-class or upper income neighborhoods. Those who charge these higher prices have been accused of "exploitation," "discrimination" and the like. But the question is whether these prices *cause* costs to be higher in low income neighborhoods or are *conveying* costs that are already higher in those neighborhoods, such as higher costs of theft, vandalism, robbery, riots, and the higher costs of security precautions and insurance to guard against these things.

If the higher prices were simply ways of earning higher rates of profit, it would be hard to explain why so many businesses avoid locating in neighborhoods where profit rates would presumably be higher, but where there is in fact usually a great lack of the number and variety of stores found in other neighborhoods. Empirical data indicate no higher profit rates in low-income minority neighborhoods,[17] which suggests that the higher prices charged there are *conveying* higher costs, not *causing* them, however much local "leaders," activists, politicians, and even intellectuals elsewhere, may prefer to blame those who charge the higher prices which reflect the higher costs of doing business.

Where those who charge the higher prices are of a different race than their neighborhood customers, then all the incentives are to blame the outsiders who *convey* higher costs, rather than those locals who *cause* them to be higher. For intellectuals, the incentives are to prefer a moral melodrama, starring themselves on the side of the angels against the forces of evil, rather than a mundane case of elementary economics that would leave intellectuals largely irrelevant. Since misdiagnosed problems are less likely to be solved, there is a high price paid by the majority of local residents, who are usually neither criminals nor rioters, for the actions of those who are. To the extent that the race industry promotes automatic solidarity based on race, rather than behavior, the majority of people in low-income minority neighborhoods may have no idea how much their solidarity with cost-creating local elements is costing them. These costs can include not only higher prices and a dearth of local businesses and professionals, but also a reluctance of taxis to take people to those neighborhoods or of various businesses to deliver in those neighborhoods.

In the more general case of disparate impacts caused by differing standards of behavior or performance, those who are subjected to standards and those who create the standards are not necessarily the most important people affected by the results. Medical schools, for example, have standards— whether for admission or for passing courses— which affect innumerable people outside the medical profession, people whose health and survival depend on the quality of medical care they receive after medical school students become doctors.

In the legal system, "disparate impact" dogma has been a gold mine for the race industry. When an employer's mix of employees shows an "underrepresentation" of designated minorities (or women), either in general or in more advanced positions, that is taken as *prima facie* evidence of discrimination, whether deliberate or as a result of using criteria with a "disparate impact" on particular groups. Another way of saying the same thing is that different groups may fail to meet relevant standards for any number of possible reasons. But the burden of proof is put on the accused employer, rather than on those doing the accusing, contrary to legal practice in most other civil or criminal cases.

No speck of evidence is required from those who implicitly assume that employee composition would be similar to population composition, in the absence of discrimination. Moreover, not one flesh-and-blood human being who even claims to have been discriminated against is necessary for "disparate impact" cases to go forward in a costly legal process. Statistics alone are sufficient to establish the "disparate impact" case that employers must rebut. Moreover, the vast financial resources available to government agencies such as the Equal Employment Opportunity Commission means that, even if an employer is exonerated after a trial, the EEOC can keep appealing the decision in successive courts, in a process that can take years and drain millions of dollars in legal expenses from the accused employer.

In a "disparate impact" case against the Sears department store chain, for example, legal processes dragged on for 15 years and cost Sears $20 million, even though there was not one past or present employee of Sears who claimed discrimination (sex discrimination in this case).[18] All that the EEOC needed to keep this financially draining process going were statistics that did not match its preconceptions. Sears eventually won in the 7th Circuit Court of Appeals, but few employers can afford millions of dollars in legal costs, quite aside from years of bad publicity based on unsubstantiated charges of discrimination. A racial discrimination case against the Wards Cove Packing Company likewise dragged on for 15 years and, even though the Supreme Court refused to accept a lower court decision against Wards Cove, based on putting the burden of proof on the accused, Congress passed a law restoring the burden of proof on the employer in civil rights cases.[19]

Given the enormous costs that can be imposed by charges of discrimination based on "disparate impact" statistics, even large employers usually find it prudent to settle such cases out of court on whatever terms they can negotiate. Although these out of court settlements are not an admission of guilt, they are widely cited by those in the race industry as damning evidence of pervasive discrimination requiring pervasive government intervention to protect supposed victims, even when there is not one identifiable victim even claiming to have been discriminated against.

Where an employer is in an industry that is already one subject to government regulatory agencies, whose permission is necessary to engage in ordinary business transactions that unregulated businesses are free to make on their own, the leverage of the government is even more powerful. This means that wholly unsubstantiated charges of discrimination can paralyze the ability of a regulated firm to make transactions on which millions, or even billions, of dollars depend, until such indefinite time as the charges have been adjudicated to the satisfaction of the regulatory agency involved. Thus banks accused of either employee discrimination or discriminatory lending practices have had their plans for opening new branches, or merging with other banks, put on hold by government regulatory agencies at the sole discretion of these agencies, without any trial, much less proof, of the charges.

Under these conditions, individuals like Jesse Jackson or organizations such as ACORN can make, and have made, charges of discrimination at virtually no cost to themselves, but which impose huge costs on the accused banks. Given these conditions, banks have paid millions of dollars to their accusers, who then withdraw their accusations, so that normal business processes can proceed in the regulated banks.[20] One economist wrote an essay on this practice titled, "How to Rob a Bank Legally."[21]

Intellectuals may think of disparate impact theory as something to discuss around a seminar table or in academic journals but, in the real world, this theory— which serves as evidence, but for which no evidence is necessary to substantiate the theory itself— is powerful leverage for transferring vast sums of money from those who earned it to those in the race industry. In a decade, more than a trillion dollars have been extracted from financial and other business organizations by community activist organizations, using a variety of tactics, according to the National Community Reinvestment Coalition.[22]

However beneficial this may have been to the race industry, among the concessions that have been won from banks have been mortgage loans made to low income and minority borrowers who would not otherwise qualify under traditional lending standards. These loans in many cases ended up leaving these borrowers with foreclosed homes and ruined credit records. As in other contexts, the race industry benefits, even when the ostensible beneficiaries of their work do not.

PROSPECTS AND PERILS

A crucial fact about the theories and social visions of intellectuals is that the intelligentsia pay no price for being wrong. In an economy where mistaken business decisions can lead to bankruptcy and extinction, even for the largest corporations, and in a political system where individuals elected to high office on a wave of enthusiasm can find themselves unceremoniously voted out of office in disgrace at the next election, the insulation of intellectuals from paying a price for the consequences of their ideas on millions of other people is a remarkable situation— one buttressed by concepts, laws and traditions ranging from freedom of the press to academic tenure to libel laws that make it nearly impossible for "public figures" to seek legal redress for even outrageous and demonstrable falsehoods about themselves in the media.

Whatever the pros and cons of these concepts, laws and traditions, the point here is simply that intellectuals are in a remarkably different position from that of other decision-makers, and that this is a fact to be taken into account when trying to understand the nature of their decisions, and especially the ability of their theories and visions to survive in defiance of empirical evidence.

Quite simply, intellectuals pay no price for being wrong, no matter how wrong or with what catastrophic consequences for millions of other people. The sweeping acceptance of theories of genetic determinism by intellectuals on both sides of the Atlantic in the early decades of the twentieth century had impacts on things ranging from immigration policies to compulsory sterilization policies to the Holocaust. Yet those who promoted these beliefs paid no price. Madison Grant's death in 1937 spared him from even learning that millions of innocent men, women and children would be systematically murdered because his book impressed Hitler.

From unaccountability to irresponsibility can be a very short step.

The point here is to suggest nothing more draconian in response than a loss of the gullibility towards ideas in vogue among the intelligentsia that can make their speculations so dangerous to others. All sorts of competing notions can be free in the marketplace of ideas, without becoming dogmas backed by the power of government, just because these notions are currently ascendant among people with high IQs and prestigious degrees and honors. All sorts of ideas, whether on race or on war or on many other subjects, have prevailed among intellectuals with results now recognized in retrospect as having been as utterly invalid intellectually as they were catastrophic in their human consequences. In other words, just because some people are justly renowned within their specialties, and may regard themselves as part of some larger class of "thinking people," does not mean that the rest of us can neglect to think for ourselves or to demand hard evidence from those with soaring visions and impressive rhetoric.

Among the ideas about race currently in vogue among the intelligentsia are some with enormous potential for needless personal and social tragedies. The apparently benign concept of "equality," with its numerous and even mutually contradictory meanings, is a fertile source of dangers to individuals, races and whole societies. Equality of treatment by the law, for example, is very different from equality of economic outcomes, and equality of potentialities is very different from equality of developed capabilities. The ease with which many among the intelligentsia turn inequalities of results into "inequities" or "discrimination" might suggest that equality is so automatic that its absence is what needs to be explained— and corrected— despite the gross inequalities in achievements and prosperity that have been common in countries around the world and for centuries of recorded history, even in circumstances in which those more fortunate have had no power to discriminate against those who were less fortunate.

The ultimate sources of these group differences in achievements can be many, and often originated in differences in skills, cultures and other circumstances inherited from past generations. But tracing these sources of intergroup differences can be an arduous and uncertain process, and one with little emotional or other payoff. Instead, those with good fortune have often attributed that good fortune to their own inherent superiority, while those less fortunate have often preferred to believe that their lesser place in the world is the result of evil done to them by others. Whole ideologies and movements can be, and have been, built on these premises— and whole nations ruined by them. Intellectuals have all too often played a major role in promoting a sense of grievance over inequalities.

The kind of society to which that can lead is one in which a newborn baby enters the world supplied with prepackaged grievances against other babies born the same day. It is hard to imagine anything more conducive to unending internal strife and a weakening of the bonds that hold a society together. When history shows how hard it can be to maintain peace and cooperation among contemporaries, why would we take on the complex, divisive and ultimately futile task of redressing issues between our long dead ancestors or pass on to generations yet unborn the seeds of strife to blight their lives?

The kind of equality being pursued by intellectuals is often the kind of equality that can be imposed unilaterally from the top down, an equality of outcomes— essentially an equality of effects without an equality of causes, or on sheer presumption of an equality of causes, in defiance of both history and logic. Even more ambitious are attempts to create equality of outcomes where differences in causes are acknowledged, but differences in effects are proposed to be eliminated by compensatory policies— a proposition advocated by Condorcet back in the eighteenth century and by Rawls in the twentieth century.[23] The actual track record of group preference policies, whether in the United States or in other countries around the world, undermines the optimistic assumption that greater equality can be produced in that way, and raises painful questions about the polarization that has all too often been produced instead.

Many people who advocate what they think of as equality promote what is in fact make-believe "equality." In economic terms, taking what others have produced and giving it to those who have not produced as much (or at all, in some cases) is make-believe equality— as contrasted with real equality, which would be enabling the less productive to become more productive, so that they could create for themselves what they are trying to take from others. However, real equality is not only harder to achieve, it is something whose achievement cannot be created by outsiders, as redistribution can be, but requires the efforts of those who lag. Make-believe equality, by creating a sense of entitlement to what others have created, reduces the incentives to making efforts to produce for one's self.

Many of what are called social problems are differences between the theories of intellectuals and the realities of the world— differences which many intellectuals interpret to mean that it is the real world that is wrong and needs changing. Apparently their theories, and the visions behind them, cannot be wrong.

None of this means that economic or other inequalities must be supinely accepted. The rise of groups from dire poverty to affluence— the Chinese in Southeast Asian countries, the Lebanese in West Africa, and Jews in the United States, among many others— shows that history is not destiny. But these rises have almost invariably been achieved in mundane and often arduous ways that not only differ from the ways advocated by the intelligentsia, but have often been in ways directly opposite to the more dramatic and emotionally satisfying ways envisioned by the intelligentsia. Moreover, earned achievements, whether modest or spectacular, bring a self respect, as well as respect from others, that can seldom be gotten from even a successful playing of a parasitic role in the name of a make-believe "equality."

NOTES

Epigraph

G. M. Trevelyan, *English Social History: A Survey of Six Centuries, Chaucer to Queen Victoria* (London: Longmans, Green and Co., 1942), p. 339.

Chapter 1: Questions About Race

1. Donald L. Niewyk, *The Jews in Weimar Germany* (Baton Rouge: Louisiana State University Press, 1980), p. 98; Raphael Patai, *The Vanished Worlds of Jewry* (New York: Macmillan, 1980), p. 57.

2. E. Franklin Frazier, "The Failure of the Negro Intellectual," *E. Franklin Frazier on Race Relations: Selected Writings*, edited by G. Franklin Edwards (Chicago: University of Chicago Press, 1968), p. 274.

3. Rochelle Sharpe, "Losing Ground: In Latest Recession, Only Blacks Suffered Net Employment Loss," *Wall Street Journal*, September 14, 1993, p. A12.

4. United States Commission on Civil Rights, *Civil Rights and the Mortgage Crisis* (Washington: U.S. Commission on Civil Rights, 2009), p. 53.

5. Board of Governors of the Federal Reserve System, *Report to the Congress on Credit Scoring and Its Effects on the Availability and Affordability of Credit*, submitted to the Congress pursuant to Section 215 of the Fair and Accurate Credit Transactions Act of 2003, August 2007, p. 80.

6. Harold A. Black, et al., "Do Black-Owned Banks Discriminate against Black Borrowers?" *Journal of Financial Services Research*, February 1997, pp. 185–200.

7. Daniel J. Losen and Jonathan Gillespie, *Opportunities Suspended: The Disparate Impact of Disciplinary Exclusion from School*, The Center for Civil Rights Remedies at The Civil Rights Project, August 2012, pp. 7, 15.

8. Sharon Noguchi, "Report: Ravenswood Has Nation's Highest Suspension Rates for Asian/Pacific Islander Students," *Contra Costa Times* (online), August 8, 2012.

9. "Enrollment in California Public School Districts," downloaded from the website of the California Department of Education at http://www.cde.ca.gov/ds/sd/cb/dataquest.asp on August 10, 2012.

Chapter 2: Disparities and Their Causes

1. Charles Issawi, "The Transformation of the Economic Position of the *Millets* in the Nineteenth Century," *Christians and Jews in the Ottoman Empire: The*

Functioning of a Plural Society, edited by Benjamin Braude and Bernard Lewis (New York: Holmes and Meier, 1982), Vol. I: *The Central Lands*, pp. 262–263.

2. Bernard Lewis, *The Jews of Islam* (Princeton: Princeton University Press, 1984), p. 214.

3. Yuan-li Wu and Chun-hsi Wu, *Economic Development in Southeast Asia: The Chinese Dimension* (Stanford: Hoover Institution Press, 1980), p. 51.

4. R. Bayly Winder, "The Lebanese in West Africa," *Comparative Studies in Society and History*, Vol. IV (1961–62), p. 309.

5. Charles Issawi, "The Transformation of the Economic Position of the *Millets* in the Nineteenth Century," *Christians and Jews in the Ottoman Empire*, edited by Benjamin Braude and Bernard Lewis, Vol. I: *The Central Lands*, pp. 262–263, 266.

6. Winthrop R. Wright, *British-Owned Railways in Argentina: Their Effect on Economic Nationalism, 1854–1948* (Austin: University of Texas Press, 1974).

7. John P. McKay, *Pioneers for Profit: Foreign Entrepreneurship and Russian Industrialization 1885–1913* (Chicago: University of Chicago Press, 1970), p. 35.

8. Jonathan I. Israel, *European Jewry in the Age of Mercantilism 1550–1750* (Oxford: Clarendon Press, 1985), p. 139.

9. Carl Solberg, *Immigration and Nationalism: Argentina and Chile, 1890–1914* (Austin: University of Texas Press, 1970), p. 68.

10. S. J. Thambiah, "Ethnic Representation in Ceylon's Higher Administrative Services, 1870–1946," *University of Ceylon Review*, Vol. 13 (April-July 1955), p. 130.

11. Lyle Spatz, *The SABR Baseball List & Record Book* (New York: Scribner, 2007), p. 335.

12. Jean Roche, *La Colonisation Allemande et le Rio Grande do Sul* (Paris: Institut Des Hautes Études de L'Amérique Latine, 1959), pp. 388–389.

13. James L. Tigner, "Japanese Immigration into Latin America: A Survey," *Journal of Interamerican Studies and World Affairs*, November 1981, p. 476.

14. H.L. van der Laan, *The Lebanese Traders in Sierra Leone* (The Hague: Mouton & Co., 1975), p. 65.

15. Ibid., p. 137.

16. Ezra Mendelsohn, *The Jews of East Central Europe between the World Wars* (Bloomington: Indiana University Press, 1983), pp. 23, 26.

17. Haraprasad Chattopadhyaya, *Indians in Africa: A Socio-Economic Study* (Calcutta: Bookland Private Limited, 1970), p. 394.

18. Haraprasad Chattopadhyaya, *Indians in Sri Lanka: A Historical Study* (Calcutta: O.P.S. Publishers Private Ltd., 1979), pp. 143, 144, 146.

19. Carl Solberg, *Immigration and Nationalism*, p. 50.

20. Felice A. Bonadio, *A.P. Giannini: Banker of America* (Berkeley: University of California Press, 1994), p. 28.

21. W.D. Borrie, *Italians and Germans in Australia: A Study of Assimilation* (Melbourne: The Australian National University, 1954), p. 106.

22. Carl Solberg, *Immigration and Nationalism*, p. 63.

23. Pablo Macera and Shane J. Hunt, "Peru," *Latin America: A Guide to Economic History 1830–1930*, edited by Roberto Cortés Conde and Stanley J. Stein (Berkeley: University of California Press, 1977), p. 565.

24. Carlo M. Cipolla, *Clocks and Culture: 1300–1700* (New York: W. W. Norton & Co., 1978), p. 68.

25. Nena Vreeland, et al., *Area Handbook for Malaysia*, third edition (Washington: U. S. Government Printing Office, 1977), p. 303.

26. Winthrop R. Wright, *British-Owned Railways in Argentina;* Gino Germani, "Mass Immigration and Modernization in Argentina," *Studies in Comparative International Development*, Vol. 2 (1966), p. 170.

27. John P. McKay, *Pioneers for Profit*, pp. 33, 34, 35.

28. Jean W. Sedlar, *East Central Europe in the Middle Ages, 1000–1500* (Seattle: University of Washington Press, 1994), p. 131.

29. Charles Issawi, "The Transformation of the Economic Position of the *Millets* in the Nineteenth Century," *Christians and Jews in the Ottoman Empire*, edited by Benjamin Braude and Bernard Lewis, Vol. I: *The Central Lands*, pp. 262, 263, 265, 266, 267.

30. Victor Purcell, *The Chinese in Southeast Asia*, second edition (Kuala Lumpur: Oxford University Press, 1980), pp. 7, 68, 83, 180, 245, 248, 540, 559.

31. Arthur Herman, *How the Scots Invented the Modern World* (New York: Crown Publishers, 2001), Chapter 5; Maldwyn A. Jones, "Ulster Emigration, 1783–1815," *Essays in Scotch-Irish History*, edited by E. R. R. Green (London: Routledge & Kegan Paul, 1969), p. 49; Eric Richards, "Australia and the Scottish Connection 1788–1914," *The Scots Abroad: Labour, Capital,*

Enterprise, 1750–1914, edited by R. A. Cage (London: Croom Helm, 1984), p. 122; E. Richards, "Highland and Gaelic Immigrants," *The Australian People*, edited by James Jupp (North Ryde, Australia: Angus & Robertson, 1988), pp. 765–769.

32. Philip E. Vernon, *Intelligence and Cultural Environment* (London: Methuen & Co., Ltd., 1970), pp. 157–158.

33. Nathan Glazer and Daniel Patrick Moynihan, *Beyond the Melting Pot: The Negroes, Puerto Ricans, Jews, Italians, and Irish of New York City*, second edition (Cambridge, Massachusetts: MIT Press, 1963), pp. 257–258; Andrew M. Greeley, *That Most Distressful Nation: The Taming of the American Irish* (Chicago: Quadrangle Books, 1972), p. 132.

34. Vladimir G. Treml, *Alcohol in the USSR: A Statistical Study* (Durham, NC: Duke University Press, 1982), p. 73.

35. Mohamed Suffian bin Hashim, "Problems and Issues of Higher Education Development in Malaysia," *Development of Higher Education in Southeast Asia: Problems and Issues*, edited by Yip Yat Hoong (Singapore: Regional Institute of Higher Education and Development, 1973), Table 8, pp. 70–71.

36. Robert J. Sharer, *The Ancient Maya*, fifth edition (Stanford: Stanford University Press, 1994), p. 455.

37. See, for example, Roy E.H. Mellor and E. Alistair Smith, *Europe: A Geographical Survey of the Continent* (New York: Columbia University Press, 1979), pp. 1–17; Norman J.G. Pounds, *An Historical Geography of Europe: 1800–1914* (Cambridge: Cambridge University Press, 1985), pp. 37–65; Jocelyn Murray, editor, *Cultural Atlas of Africa* (New York: Facts on File Publications, 1981), pp. 10–22; Thomas Sowell, *Conquests and Cultures: An International History* (New York: Basic Books, 1998), pp. 99–109.

38. J. F. Ade Ajayi and Michael Crowder, editors, *Historical Atlas of Africa* (Cambridge: Cambridge University Press, 1985), Section 2; Kathleen Baker, "The Changing Geography of West Africa," *The Changing Geography of Africa and the Middle East*, edited by Graham P. Chapman and Kathleen M. Baker (London: Routledge, 1992), p. 105.

39. Fernand Braudel, *The Mediterranean and the Mediterranean World in the Age of Philip II*, translated by Siân Reynolds (Berkeley: University of California Press, 1995), Vol. I, p. 35.

40. William S. Maltby, *The Rise and Fall of the Spanish Empire* (New York: Palgrave Macmillan, 2009), p. 18; Peter Pierson, *The History of Spain* (Westport, CT: Greenwood Press, 1999), pp. 7–8.

41. John H. Chambers, *A Traveller's History of Australia* (New York: Interlink Books, 1999), pp. 22–24.

42. H. J. de Blij and Peter O. Muller, *Geography: Regions and Concepts,* sixth edition (New York: John Wiley & Sons, Inc., 1992), p. 394.

43. Oscar Handlin, "Introduction," *The Positive Contribution by Immigrants* (Paris: United Nations Educational, Scientific and Cultural Organization, 1955), p. 13.

44. Ulrich Bonnell Phillips, *The Slave Economy of the Old South: Selected Essays in Economic and Social History*, edited by Eugene D. Genovese (Baton Rouge: Louisiana State University Press, 1968), p. 269.

45. See, for example, Thomas Sowell, *Conquests and Cultures*, pp. 175–176.

46. See, for example, "We're Doing All Right, But What About You?" *The Economist*, August 16, 2003, p. 43. Russia has a Gross Domestic Product per capita that is less than half that of Britain, France or Germany and less than one-third that of Norway or Luxembourg. The Economist, *Pocket World in Figures*, 2011 edition (London: Profile Books, Ltd., 2010), p. 27. Meanwhile, the per capita income of black Americans is 64 percent of that of white Americans. Carmen DeNavas-Walt, et al., "Income, Poverty, and Health Insurance Coverage in the United States: 2009," *Current Population Reports*, P60–238 (Washington: US Census Bureau, 2010), p. 6.

47. Angelo M. Codevilla, *The Character of Nations: How Politics Makes and Breaks Prosperity, Family, and Civility* (New York: Basic Books, 1997), p. 50.

48. See Thomas Sowell, *Conquests and Cultures*, pp. 177–184.

49. Robert Bartlett, *The Making of Europe: Conquest, Colonization and Cultural Change, 950–1350* (Princeton: Princeton University Press, 1993), p. 235.

50. Jean W. Sedlar, *East Central Europe in the Middle Ages, 1000–1500*, pp. 126–127.

51. Stephen Steinberg, *The Ethnic Myth: Race, Ethnicity, and Class in America* (New York: Atheneum, 1981), pp. 99–103.

52. See, for example, U.S. Bureau of the Census, *We the People: Asians in the United States*, Census 2000 Special Reports, December 2004, p. 6; U.S. Bureau of the Census, *We the People: Hispanics in the United States*, Census 2000 Special

Reports, December 2004, p. 5; U.S. Bureau of the Census, *We the People: Blacks in the United States,* Census 2000 Special Reports, August 2005, p. 4.

53.   U.S. Bureau of the Census, *We the People: Asians in the United States*, Census 2000 Special Reports, December 2004, p. 6.

54.   The Economist, *Pocket World in Figures*, 2011 edition, p. 18.

55.   Oscar Handlin, *Boston's Immigrants* (New York: Atheneum, 1970), p. 114.

56.   Carl Wittke, *The Irish in America* (New York: Russell & Russell, 1970), p. 101; Oscar Handlin, *Boston's Immigrants*, pp. 169–170; Jay P. Dolan, *The Irish Americans: A History* (New York: Bloomsbury Press, 2008), pp. 118–119.

57.   Arthur R. Jensen, "How Much Can We Boost IQ and Scholastic Achievement?" *Harvard Educational Review*, Vol. 39, No. 1 (Winter 1969), p. 35; Richard J. Herrnstein and Charles Murray, *The Bell Curve: Intelligence and Class Structure in American Life* (New York: The Free Press, 1994), p. 110.

58.   Edward C. Banfield, *The Unheavenly City*, revised edition (Boston: Little, Brown and Company, 1974), p. 91.

59.   Moses Rischin, *The Promised City: New York's Jews 1870–1914* (Cambridge, Massachusetts: Harvard University Press, 1962), p. 76.

60.   Louis Wirth, *The Ghetto* (Chicago: University of Chicago Press, 1964), pp. 204–205.

61.   E. Franklin Frazier, "The Impact of Urban Civilization Upon Negro Family Life," *American Sociological Review*, Vol. 2, No. 5 (October 1937), p. 615.

62.   Jonathan Gill, *Harlem: The Four Hundred Year History from Dutch Village to Capital of Black America* (New York: Grove Press, 2011), p. 284.

63.   Ibid., p. 140.

64.   Robert F. Foerster, *The Italian Emigration of Our Times* (New York: Arno Press, 1969), p. 393; Dino Cinel, *From Italy to San Francisco: The Immigrant Experience* (Stanford: Stanford University Press, 1982), p. 28.

65.   Samuel L. Baily, "The Adjustment of Italian Immigrants in Buenos Aires and New York, 1870–1914," *American Historical Review*, April 1983, p. 291; John E. Zucchi, *Italians in Toronto: Development of a National Identity, 1875–1935* (Kingston, Ontario: McGill-Queen's University Press, 1988), pp. 41, 53–55, 58.

66.   Lawrence E. Harrison, *Underdevelopment Is a State of Mind: The Latin American Case* (Cambridge, Massachusetts: Center for International Affairs, Harvard University, 1985), p. 164.

Chapter 3: Changing Racial Beliefs

1. See, for example, various chapter titles in Madison Grant, *The Passing of the Great Race or the Racial Basis of European History*, revised edition (New York: Charles Scribner's Sons, 1918).

2. Ibid., p. 16.

3. Mark H. Haller, *Eugenics: Hereditarian Attitudes in American Thought* (New Brunswick: Rutgers University Press, 1963), p. 11.

4. Madison Grant, *The Passing of the Great Race*, revised edition, p. 100. The book was a best-seller according to Paul Johnson, *Modern Times: The World from the Twenties to the Nineties*, revised edition (New York: Perennial Classics, 2001), p. 203.

5. Reports of the Immigration Commission, *The Children of Immigrants in Schools* (Washington: Government Printing Office, 1911), Vol. I, p. 110.

6. Carl C. Brigham, *A Study of American Intelligence* (Princeton: Princeton University Press, 1923), p. xx.

7. Ibid., p. 119.

8. Robert M. Yerkes, *Psychological Examining in the United States Army*, Memoirs of the National Academy of Sciences (Washington: Government Printing Office, 1921), Vol. 15, pp. 123–292; Carl C. Brigham, *A Study of American Intelligence*, pp. 80, 121.

9. Rudolph Pintner and Ruth Keller, "Intelligence Tests of Foreign Children," *Journal of Educational Psychology*, Vol. 13, Issue 4 (April 1922), p. 215.

10. Nathaniel D. Mttron Hirsch, "A Study of Natio-Racial Mental Differences," *Genetic Psychology Monographs*, Vol. 1, Nos. 3 and 4 (May and July, 1926), p. 302.

11. Otto Klineberg, *Race Differences* (New York: Harper & Brothers, 1935), pp. 183–184.

12. Ibid., p. 182. For critiques of the World War I data, from differing points of view, see Audrey M. Shuey, *The Testing of Negro Intelligence*, second edition (New York: Social Science Press, 1966), pp. 310–311; Carl C. Brigham, "Intelligence Tests of Immigrant Groups," *Psychological Review*, Vol. 37, Issue 2 (March 1930); Thomas Sowell, "Race and IQ Reconsidered," *Essays and Data on American Ethnic Groups*, edited by Thomas Sowell and Lynn D. Collins (Washington: The Urban Institute, 1978), pp. 226–227.

13. Carl C. Brigham, *A Study of American Intelligence*, p. 190.

14. H.H. Goddard, "The Binet Tests in Relation to Immigration," *Journal of Psycho-Asthenics*, Vol. 18, No. 2 (December 1913), p. 110.

15. Quoted in Leon J. Kamin, *The Science and Politics of I.Q.* (New York: John Wiley and Sons, 1974), p. 6.

16. Carl Brigham, for example, said, "The decline of American intelligence will be more rapid than the decline of the intelligence of European national groups, owing to the presence here of the negro." Carl C. Brigham, *A Study of American Intelligence*, p. 210.

17. "The Control of Births," *New Republic*, March 6, 1915, p. 114.

18. Sidney Webb, "Eugenics and the Poor Law: The Minority Report," *Eugenics Review*, Vol. II (April 1910-January 1911), p. 240; Thomas C. Leonard, "Eugenics and Economics in the Progressive Era," *Journal of Economic Perspectives*, Vol. 19, No. 4 (Fall 2005), p. 216.

19. Richard Overy, *The Twilight Years: The Paradox of Britain Between the Wars* (New York: Viking, 2009), pp. 93, 105, 106, 107, 124–127.

20. Matthew Pratt Guterl, *The Color of Race in America: 1900–1940* (Cambridge, Massachusetts: Harvard University Press, 2001), p. 67.

21. Madison Grant, *The Passing of the Great Race*, revised edition, p. 17.

22. Ibid., p. 48.

23. Ibid., p. 60.

24. Ibid., p. 77.

25. Ibid., p. 32.

26. Ibid., p. 19.

27. Ibid., p. 20.

28. Ibid., p. 104.

29. Ibid., p. 257.

30. Ibid., p. 258.

31. Ibid., p. 260.

32. Ibid., p. 101.

33. Ibid., p. 105.

34. Ibid., p. xxi.

35. Ibid., p. 49.

36. Ibid., p. 58.

37. Ibid., p. 59.

38. Ibid., p. 89.

39. Ibid., p. 16.

40. Ibid., p. 91.

41. Ibid., p. 263.

42. Jonathan Peter Spiro, *Defending the Master Race: Conservation, Eugenics, and the Legacy of Madison Grant* (Burlington: University of Vermont Press, 2009), pp. 6, 10, 17, 22–34.

43. "Scientific Books," *Science*, Vol. 48, No. 1243 (October 25, 1918), p. 419.

44. Madison Grant, *The Conquest of a Continent or the Expansion of Races in America* (York, SC: Liberty Bell Publications, 2004), p. xii.

45. Jonathan Peter Spiro, *Defending the Master Race*, pp. 98, 99.

46. Edward Alsworth Ross, *The Principles of Sociology* (New York: The Century Co., 1920), p. 63.

47. Edward Alsworth Ross, "Who Outbreeds Whom?" *Proceedings of the Third Race Betterment Conference* (Battle Creek, Michigan: Race Betterment Foundation, 1928), p. 77.

48. Edward Alsworth Ross, *The Old World in the New: The Significance of Past and Present Immigration to the American People* (New York: The Century Company, 1914), pp. 285–286.

49. Ibid., p. 288.

50. Ibid., pp. 288–289.

51. Ibid., p. 293.

52. Ibid., p. 295.

53. "Social Darwinism," *American Journal of Sociology*, Vol. 12, No. 5 (March 1907), p. 715.

54. Edward A. Ross, "The Causes of Race Superiority," *Annals of the American Academy of Political and Social Science*, Vol. 18 (July 1901), p. 89.

55. Ibid., p. 85.

56. Francis A. Walker, "Methods of Restricting Immigration," *Discussions in Economics and Statistics*, Volume II: *Statistics, National Growth, Social Economics*, edited by Davis R. Dewey (New York: Henry Holt and Company, 1899), p. 430.

57. Ibid., p. 432.

58. Francis A. Walker, "Restriction of Immigration," Ibid., p. 438.

59. Ibid., p. 447.
60. Thomas C. Leonard, "Eugenics and Economics in the Progressive Era," *Journal of Economic Perspectives*, Vol. 19, No. 4 (Fall 2005), p. 211.
61. *Annual Report of the Commissioner of Indian Affairs to the Secretary of the Interior for the Year 1872* (Washington: Government Printing Office, 1872), p. 11.
62. Richard T. Ely, "Fraternalism vs. Paternalism in Government," *The Century Magazine*, Vol. 55, No. 5 (March 1898), p. 781.
63. Richard T. Ely, "The Price of Progress," *Administration*, Vol. III, No. 6 (June 1922), p. 662.
64. Sidney Fine, "Richard T. Ely, Forerunner of Progressivism, 1880–1901," *Mississippi Valley Historical Review*, Vol. 37, No. 4 (March 1951), pp. 604, 609.
65. Ibid., p. 610.
66. Ibid., p. 603.
67. "Dr. R.T. Ely Dies; Noted Economist," *New York Times*, October 5, 1943, p. 25; Richard T. Ely, "Fraternalism vs. Paternalism in Government," *The Century Magazine*, Vol. 55, No. 5 (March 1898), p. 784.
68. "Dr. R.T. Ely Dies; Noted Economist," *New York Times*, October 5, 1943, p. 25.
69. Thomas C. Leonard, "Eugenics and Economics in the Progressive Era," *Journal of Economic Perspectives*, Vol. 19, No. 4 (Fall 2005), p. 215.
70. Ibid., p. 214.
71. Ibid., p. 221.
72. Ibid., p. 212.
73. Ibid., p. 213.
74. Ibid., p. 216.
75. Ibid.
76. William E. Spellman, "The Economics of Edward Alsworth Ross," *American Journal of Economics and Sociology*, Vol. 38, No. 2 (April 1979), pp. 129–140; Howard W. Odum, "Edward Alsworth Ross: 1866–1951," *Social Forces*, Vol. 30, No. 1 (October 1951), pp. 126–127; John L. Gillin, "In Memoriam: Edward Alsworth Ross," *The Midwest Sociologist*, Vol. 14, No. 1 (Fall 1951), p. 18.
77. Edward Alsworth Ross, *Seventy Years of It: An Autobiography* (New York: D. Appleton-Century Company, 1936), pp. 97–98.
78. Julius Weinberg, *Edward Alsworth Ross and the Sociology of Progressivism* (Madison: The State Historical Society of Wisconsin, 1972), p. 136.

79. William E. Spellman, "The Economics of Edward Alsworth Ross," *American Journal of Economics and Sociology*, Vol. 38, No. 2 (April 1979), p. 130.

80. Edward Alsworth Ross, *Sin and Society: An Analysis of Latter-Day Iniquity* (Boston: Houghton-Mifflin Company, 1907), pp. ix–xi.

81. Edward Alsworth Ross, *Seventy Years of It*, p. 98.

82. Henry C. Taylor, "Richard Theodore Ely: April 13, 1854-October 4, 1943," *The Economic Journal*, Vol. 54, No. 213 (April 1944), p. 133; "Dr. R.T. Ely Dies; Noted Economist," *New York Times*, October 5, 1943, p. 25.

83. Henry C. Taylor, "Richard Theodore Ely: April 13, 1854-October 4, 1943," *The Economic Journal*, Vol. 54, No. 213 (April 1944), p. 133.

84. Ibid., p. 134.

85. Ibid., p. 137.

86. Henry C. Taylor, "Richard Theodore Ely: April 13, 1854-October 4, 1943," *The Economic Journal*, Vol. 54, No. 213 (April 1944), pp. 132–138.

87. George McDaniel, "Madison Grant and the Racialist Movement," in Madison Grant, *The Conquest of a Continent*, p. iv.

88. Jonathan Peter Spiro, *Defending the Master Race*, pp. xv–xvi.

89. Ibid., p. 17.

90. Ibid., p. 250.

91. Jan Cohn, *Creating America: George Horace Lorimer and the Saturday Evening Post* (Pittsburgh: University of Pittsburgh Press, 1989), p. 5.

92. Ibid., pp. 49, 92, 95–96.

93. Ibid., p. 155.

94. "The Great American Myth," *Saturday Evening Post*, May 7, 1921, p. 20.

95. Kenneth L. Roberts, "Lest We Forget," *Saturday Evening Post*, April 28, 1923, pp. 158, 162.

96. Kenneth L. Roberts, *Why Europe Leaves Home* (Bobbs-Merrill Company, 1922), p. 15.

97. Ibid., p. 21.

98. Ibid., p. 22.

99. Ibid., p. 119.

100. Kenneth L. Roberts, "Slow Poison," *Saturday Evening Post*, February 2, 1924, p. 9.

101. George Creel, "Melting Pot or Dumping Ground?" *Collier's*, September 3, 1921, p. 10.

102. Ibid., p. 26.

103. George Creel, "Close the Gates!" *Collier's*, May 6, 1922, p. 10.

104. Henry L. Mencken, *The Philosophy of Friedrich Nietzsche* (Boston: Luce and Company, 1908), pp. 167–168.

105. "Mencken's Reply to La Monte's Fourth Letter," *Men versus The Man: A Correspondence Between Robert Rives La Monte, Socialist and H.L. Mencken, Individualist* (New York: Henry Holt and Company, 1910), p. 162.

106. H.L. Mencken, "The Aframerican: New Style," *The American Mercury*, February 1926, pp. 254, 255.

107. Ibid., p. 255.

108. H.L. Mencken, "Utopia by Sterilization," *The American Mercury*, August 1937, pp. 399, 408.

109. H.G. Wells, *The Work, Wealth and Happiness of Mankind* (Garden City, NY: Doubleday, Doran & Company, 1931), pp. 733, 734, 746.

110. H.G. Wells, *What Is Coming?: A European Forecast* (New York: The Macmillan Company, 1916), p. 254.

111. Jack London, *The Unpublished and Uncollected Articles and Essays*, edited by Daniel J. Wichlan (Bloomington, IN: AuthorHouse, 2007), pp. 60, 66.

112. George McDaniel, "Madison Grant and the Racialist Movement," in Madison Grant, *The Conquest of a Continent*, p. ii.

113. Arthur S. Link, *Woodrow Wilson and the Progressive Era: 1910–1917* (New York: Harper & Brothers Publishers, 1954), pp. 64–66. The number of black postmasters declined from 153 in 1910 to 78 in 1930. Gunnar Myrdal, *An American Dilemma: The Negro Problem and Modern Democracy* (New York: Harper & Brothers Publishers, 1944), p. 327. See also Henry Blumenthal, "Woodrow Wilson and the Race Question," *Journal of Negro History*, Vol. 48, No. 1 (January 1963), pp. 1–21.

114. S. Georgia Nugent, "Changing Faces: The Princeton Student of the Twentieth Century," *Princeton University Library Chronicle*, Vol. LXII, Number 2 (Winter 2001), pp. 215–216.

115. Edmund Morris, *The Rise of Theodore Roosevelt* (New York: The Modern Library, 2001), p. 483.

116. In his memoirs, looking back on his days as a police commissioner in New York, Theodore Roosevelt said: "The appointments to the police force were made as I have described in the last chapter. We paid not the slightest attention to a man's politics or creed, or where he was born, so long as he was an American citizen; and on an average we obtained far and away the best men that had ever come into the Police Department." Theodore Roosevelt, *The Rough Riders: An Autobiography* (New York: The Library of America, 2004), p. 428.

117. Edmund Morris, *Theodore Rex* (New York: Modern Library, 2002), pp. 52–53.

118. Quoted in Bernard Lewis, *The Muslim Discovery of Europe* (New York: W. W. Norton, 1982), p. 139.

119. Edward Byron Reuter, *The Mulatto in the United States* (Boston: Richard G. Badger, The Gorham Press, 1918).

120. Theodore Hershberg and Henry Williams, "Mulattoes and Blacks: Intra-group Color Differences and Social Stratification in Nineteenth-Century Philadelphia," *Philadelphia*, edited by Theodore Hershberg (New York: Oxford University Press, 1981), p. 402.

121. For examples of the latter assumption, see, for example, Michael Tonry, *Punishing Race: A Continuing American Dilemma* (New York: Oxford University Press, 2011), pp. 65–66.

122. See, for example, E. Franklin Frazier, *The Negro in the United States*, revised edition (New York: The Macmillan Co., 1957), p. 67; David W. Cohen and Jack P. Greene, "Introduction," *Neither Slave Nor Free: The Freedmen of African Descent in the Slave Societies of the New World*, edited by David W. Cohen and Jack P. Greene (Baltimore: The Johns Hopkins University Press, 1972), p. 7; A.J.R. Russell-Wood, "Colonial Brazil," Ibid., p. 91.

123. Calculated from data in *The Seventh Census of the United States: 1850* (Washington: Robert Armstrong, 1853), pp. xliii, lxi; U.S. Bureau of the Census, *Historical Statistics of the United States: Colonial Times to 1970* (Washington: Government Printing Office, 1975), Part I, p. 382.

124. Urbanization data for blacks in 1860 and 1920 calculated from data in the following sources: Wilbur Zelinsky, "The Population Geography of the Free Negro in Ante-Bellum America," *Population Studies*, Vol. 3, No. 4 (March 1950), pp. 387, 389; Reynolds Farley, "The Urbanization of Negroes in the United States," *Journal of Social History*, Vol. 1, No. 3 (Spring 1968), p. 255;

U. S. Bureau of the Census, *Historical Statistics of the United States: Colonial Times to 1970*, Part 1, pp. 8, 9, 12, 22.

125. Thomas Sowell, "Three Black Histories," *Essays and Data on American Ethnic Groups*, edited by Thomas Sowell and Lynn D. Collins, p. 12.

126. Ibid.

127. Madison Grant, *The Conquest of a Continent*, pp. 283–284.

Chapter 4: Internal Responses to Disparities

1.   James Buchan, *Crowded with Genius: The Scottish Enlightenment, Edinburgh's Moment of the Mind* (New York: HarperCollins, 2003), p. 129.

2.   See, for example, Olive and Sydney Checkland, *Industry and Ethos: Scotland 1832–1914* (Edinburgh: Edinburgh University Press, 1989), pp. 147–150; William R. Brock, *Scotus Americanus: A Survey of the Sources for Links between Scotland and America in the Eighteenth Century* (Edinburgh: Edinburgh University Press, 1982), pp. 114–115; Esmond Wright, "Education in the American Colonies: The Impact of Scotland," *Essays in Scotch-Irish History*, edited by E. R. R. Green (London: Routledge & Kegan Paul, 1969), pp. 40–41; Bruce Lenman, *Integration, Enlightenment, and Industrialization: Scotland 1746–1832* (Toronto: University of Toronto Press, 1981), p. 91.

3.   Anders Henriksson, *The Tsar's Loyal Germans: The Riga German Community: Social Change and the Nationality Question, 1855–1905* (Boulder: East European Monographs, 1983), pp. 1, 4.

4.   Ingeborg Fleischhauer, "The Germans' Role in Tsarist Russia: A Reappraisal," *The Soviet Germans*, edited by Edith Rogovin Frankel (London: C. Hurst & Company, 1986), p. 16.

5.   Anders Henriksson, *The Tsar's Loyal Germans*, p. 2.

6.   Ibid., pp. 15, 35, 54.

7.   Ibid., p. 15.

8.   Robert A. Kann and Zdeněk V. David, *The Peoples of the Eastern Habsburg Lands, 1526–1918* (Seattle: University of Washington Press, 1984), p. 201.

9.   Gary B. Cohen, *The Politics of Ethnic Survival: Germans in Prague, 1861–1914* (Princeton: Princeton University Press, 1981), p. 3.

10. Jeremy King, *Budweisers into Czechs and Germans: A Local History of Bohemian Politics, 1848–1948* (Princeton: Princeton University Press, 2005), p. 4.

11. Gary B. Cohen, *The Politics of Ethnic Survival*, Chapters 1, 2; Anders Henriksson, *The Tsar's Loyal Germans*, pp. x, 12, 34, 35, 54, 57–59, 61; Donald L. Horowitz, *Ethnic Groups in Conflict* (Berkeley: University of California Press, 1985), p. 286.

12. Gary B. Cohen, *The Politics of Ethnic Survival*, p. 28.

13. See, for example, Gunnar Myrdal, *Asian Drama: An Inquiry Into the Poverty of Nations* (New York: Pantheon, 1968), Vol. III, p. 1642.

14. Donald L. Horowitz, *Ethnic Groups in Conflict*, p. 97.

15. Leon Volovici, *Nationalist Ideology and Antisemitism: The Case of Romanian Intellectuals in the 1930s* (Oxford: Pergamon Press, 1991), p. 60.

16. Ibid., p. 14.

17. Ibid., p. 31.

18. Ibid., p. 42.

19. Mary Fainsod Katzenstein, *Ethnicity and Equality: The Shiv Sena Party and Preferential Policies in Bombay* (Ithaca: Cornell University Press, 1979), pp. 48–49; Myron Weiner and Mary Fainsod Katzenstein, *India's Preferential Policies: Migrants, the Middle Classes, and Ethnic Equality* (Chicago: University of Chicago Press, 1981), pp. 10–11, 44–46.

20. Ezra Mendelsohn, *The Jews of East Central Europe Between the World Wars* (Bloomington: Indiana University Press, 1983), pp. 98–99, 106.

21. Larry Diamond, "Class, Ethnicity, and the Democratic State: Nigeria, 1950–1966," *Comparative Studies in Society and History*, Vol. 25, No. 3 (July 1983), pp. 462, 473; Donald L. Horowitz, *Ethnic Groups in Conflict*, p. 225.

22. Anatoly M. Khazanov, "The Ethnic Problems of Contemporary Kazakhstan," *Central Asian Survey*, Vol. 14, No. 2 (1995), pp. 244, 257.

23. Leon Volovici, *National Ideology and Antisemitism, passim*; Joseph Rothschild, *East Central Europe between the Two World Wars* (Seattle: University of Washington Press, 1992), p. 293; Irina Livezeanu, *Cultural Politics in Greater Romania: Regionalism, Nation Building, & Ethnic Struggle, 1918–1930* (Ithaca: Cornell University Press, 1995), *passim*.

24. Gunnar Myrdal, *Asian Drama*, Vol. I, p. 348; Donald L. Horowitz, *Ethnic Groups in Conflict*, p. 133.

25. Conrad Black, "Canada's Continuing Identity Crisis," *Foreign Affairs*, Vol. 74, No. 2 (March-April 1995), p. 100.

26. See, for example, Gary B. Cohen, *The Politics of Ethnic Survival*, pp. 26–28, 32, 133, 236–237; Ezra Mendelsohn, *The Jews of East Central Europe Between the World Wars*, p. 167; Hugh LeCaine Agnew, *Origins of the Czech National Renascence* (Pittsburgh: University of Pittsburgh Press, 1993), *passim*.

27. William Pfaff, *The Wrath of Nations: Civilization and the Furies of Nationalism* (New York: Simon & Schuster, 1993), p. 156.

28. Maurice Pinard and Richard Hamilton, "The Class Bases of the Quebec Independence Movement: Conjectures and Evidence," *Ethnic and Racial Studies*, Volume 7, Issue 1 (January 1984), pp. 19–54.

29. Joseph Rothschild, *East Central Europe between the Two World Wars*, p. 20; Irina Livezeanu, *Cultural Politics in Greater Romania*, pp. 56, 218, 242, 298–299.

30. Irina Livezeanu, *Cultural Politics in Greater Romania*, p. 385.

31. Chandra Richard de Silva, "Sinhala-Tamil Relations and Education in Sri Lanka: The University Admissions Issue— The First Phase, 1971–7," *From Independence to Statehood: Managing Ethnic Conflict in Five African and Asian States*, edited by Robert B. Goldmann and A. Jeyaratnam Wilson (London: Frances Pinter, 1984), p. 126.

32. Warren Zimmerman, "The Last Ambassador: A Memoir of the Collapse of Yugoslavia," *Foreign Affairs*, March-April 1995, pp. 9, 17; William Pfaff, *The Wrath of Nations*, p. 55.

33. Paul Johnson, *Modern Times: The World from the Twenties to the Nineties*, revised edition (New York: Perennial Classics, 2001), pp. 654–655.

34. Quoted in William Pfaff, *The Wrath of Nations*, p. 96.

35. Myron Weiner, *Sons of the Soil: Migration and Ethnic Conflict in India* (Princeton: Princeton University Press, 1978), p. 107; Donald L. Horowitz, *Ethnic Groups in Conflict*, pp. 219–224.

36. S. J. Tambiah, *Sri Lanka: Ethnic Fratricide and the Dismantling of Democracy* (Chicago: University of Chicago Press, 1986), pp. 20–21, 26; William McGowan, *Only Man is Vile: The Tragedy of Sri Lanka* (New York: Farrar, Straus and Giroux, 1992), pp. 97, 98.

37. Joseph Rothschild, *East Central Europe between the Two World Wars*, p. 92.

38. Radomír Luža, *The Transfer of the Sudeten Germans: A Study of Czech-German Relations, 1933–1962* (New York: New York University Press, 1964), pp. 9, 11, 42.

39. Ibid., p. 34.

40. Ibid., p. 290.

41. Cacilie Rohwedder, "Germans, Czechs are Hobbled by History as Europe Moves toward United Future," *Wall Street Journal*, November 25, 1996, p. A15.

42. P.T. Bauer, *Equality, the Third World and Economic Delusion* (Cambridge, Massachusetts: Harvard University Press, 1981), pp. 70–71.

43. Michael Ornstein, *Ethno-Racial Inequality in the City of Toronto: An Analysis of the 1996 Census*, May 2000, p. ii.

44. Charles H. Young and Helen R.Y. Reid, *The Japanese Canadians* (Toronto: University of Toronto Press, 1938), pp. 9–10, 49, 53, 58, 76, 120, 129, 130, 145, 172.

45. Thomas Sowell, *Black Rednecks and White Liberals* (San Francisco: Encounter Books, 2005), p. 251.

46. Elissa Gootman, "City to Help Curb Harassment of Asian Students at High School," *New York Times*, June 2, 2004, p. B9; Joe Williams, "New Attack at Horror HS; Top Senior Jumped at Brooklyn's Troubled Lafayette," *New York Daily News*, December 7, 2002, p. 7; Maki Becker, "Asian Students Hit in Rash of HS Attacks," *New York Daily News*, December 8, 2002, p. 7; Kristen A. Graham and Jeff Gammage, "Two Immigrant Students Attacked at Bok," *Philadelphia Inquirer*, September 21, 2010, p. B1; Jeff Gammage and Kristen A. Graham, "Feds Find Merit in Asian Students' Claims Against Philly School," *Philadelphia Inquirer*, August 28, 2010, p. A1; Kristen A. Graham and Jeff Gammage, "Report Released on Racial Violence at S. Phila. High," *Philadelphia Inquirer*, February 24, 2010, p. A1; Kristen A. Graham, "Other Phila. Schools Handle Racial, Ethnic Tensions," *Philadelphia Inquirer*, February 4, 2010, p. A1; Kristen A. Graham and Jeff Gammage, "Attacking Immigrant Students Not New, Say Those Involved," *Philadelphia Inquirer*, December 18, 2009, p. B1; Kristen A. Graham, "Asian Students Describe Violence at South Philadelphia High," *Philadelphia Inquirer*, December 10, 2009, p. A1.

47. See, for example, Ian Urbina, "Mobs Are Born as Word Grows By Text Message," *New York Times*, March 25, 2010, p. A1; Kirk Mitchell, "Attacks Change Lives on All Sides," *Denver Post*, December 6, 2009, pp. A1 ff; Alan Gathright, 7News Content Producer, "Black Gangs Vented Hatred for Whites in Downtown Attacks," *The DenverChannel.com*, December 5, 2009; Meg

Jones, "Flynn Calls Looting, Beatings in Riverwest Barbaric," *Milwaukee Journal Sentinel*, July 6, 2011, pp. A1 ff; Mareesa Nicosia, "Four Skidmore College Students Charged in Assault; One Charged with Felony Hate Crime," *The Saratogian* (online), December 22, 2010; "Concealing Black Hate Crimes," *Investor's Business Daily*, August 15, 2011, p. A16; Joseph A. Slobodzian, "West Philly Man Pleads Guilty to 'Flash Mob' Assault," *Philadelphia Inquirer*, June 21, 2011, pp. B1 ff; Alfred Lubrano, "What's Behind 'Flash Mobs'?" *Philadelphia Inquirer*, March 28, 2010, pp. A1 ff; Stephanie Farr, "'Geezer' Won't Let Thugs Ruin His Walks," *Philadelphia Daily News*, October 20, 2011, Local section, p. 26; Barry Paddock and John Lauinger, "Subway Gang Attack," *New York Daily News*, July 18, 2011, News, p. 3.

Chapter 5: Race and Intelligence

1. Mark H. Haller, *Eugenics: Hereditarian Attitudes in American Thought* (New Brunswick: Rutgers University Press, 1963), p. 11.
2. Arthur R. Jensen, *Straight Talk About Mental Tests* (New York: The Free Press, 1981), p. 171. See also, Robert C. Nichols, "Heredity, Environment, and School Achievement," *Measurement and Evaluation in Guidance*, Vol. 1, No. 2 (Summer 1968), p. 126.
3. Mark H. Haller, *Eugenics*, p. 11.
4. The article was Arthur R. Jensen, "How Much Can We Boost IQ and Scholastic Achievement?" *Harvard Educational Review*, Vol. 39, No. 1 (Winter 1969). For examples of the reactions, see for example, Lawrence E. Davies, "Harassment Charged by Author of Article About Negroes' I.Q.'s," *New York Times*, May 19, 1969, p. 33; "Campus Totalitarians," *New York Times*, May 20, 1969, p. 46; "Panelists Assail View on Black I.Q.," *New York Times*, November 23, 1969, p. 88; Robert Reinhold, "Psychologist Arouses Storm by Linking I.Q. to Heredity," *New York Times*, March 30, 1969, p. 52; "Born Dumb?" *Newsweek*, March 31, 1969, p. 84; Maurice R. Berube, "Jensen's Complaint," *Commonweal*, October 10, 1969, pp. 42–44; "Intelligence and Race," *New Republic*, April 5, 1969, pp. 10–11; "The New Rage at Berkeley," *Newsweek*, June 2, 1969, p. 69; "Let There Be Darkness," *National Review*, October 7, 1969, pp. 996–997. For early intellectual responses by professionals, see *Environment, Heredity, and Intelligence*, Reprint Series No. 2, a 246-page

reprint of articles compiled from the *Harvard Educational Review*, Vol. 39, Nos. 1 and 2 (Winter and Spring 1969).

5. Arthur R. Jensen, "How Much Can We Boost IQ and Scholastic Achievement?" *Harvard Educational Review*, Winter 1969, p. 100.

6. Ibid., p. 78.

7. Ibid., p. 100.

8. Ibid., p. 95.

9. Ibid., pp. 106, 115–117.

10. Ibid., p. 117.

11. Ibid., pp. 106, 116.

12. Ibid., p. 79.

13. Ibid., p. 95.

14. James R. Flynn, *Asian Americans: Achievement Beyond IQ* (Hillsdale, NJ: Lawrence Erlbaum Associates, Publishers, 1991), p. 1.

15. Ibid., pp. 116–117.

16. Richard J. Herrnstein and Charles Murray, *The Bell Curve: Intelligence and Class Structure in American Life* (New York: The Free Press, 1994), pp. 70–74; Robert Klitgaard, *Choosing Elites* (New York: Basic Books, 1985), pp. 104–115; Stanley Sue and Jennifer Abe, *Predictors of Academic Achievement Among Asian American and White Students* (New York: College Entrance Examination Board, 1988), p. 1; Robert A. Gordon and Eileen E. Rudert, "Bad News Concerning IQ Tests," *Sociology of Education*, July 1979, p. 176; Frank L. Schmidt and John E. Hunter, "Employment Testing: Old Theories and New Research Findings," *American Psychologist*, October 1981, p. 1131; Arthur R. Jensen, "Selection of Minority Students in Higher Education," *University of Toledo Law Review*, Spring-Summer 1970, pp. 440, 443; Donald A. Rock, "Motivation, Moderators, and Test Bias," Ibid., pp. 536, 537; Ronald L. Flaugher, *Testing Practices, Minority Groups, and Higher Education: A Review and Discussion of the Research* (Princeton: Educational Testing Service, 1970), p. 11; Arthur R. Jensen, *Bias in Mental Testing* (New York: The Free Press, 1980), pp. 479–490.

17. Richard Lynn, *Race Differences in Intelligence: An Evolutionary Analysis* (Augusta, GA: Washington Summit Publishers, 2006), pp. 124–125.

18. Robert Klitgaard, *Choosing Elites*, pp. 161–165.

19. The Supreme Court said, in *Griggs v. Duke Power Company*, that any job criteria "must have a manifest relationship to the employment in question." *Griggs v. Duke Power Company*, 401 U.S. 424 (1971), at 432. But what is "manifest" to third parties with neither expertise in psychometrics nor practical experience in the particular business, much less a stake in the outcome, is something that can be known only after the fact, and is thus essentially *ex post facto* law that is expressly forbidden by the Constitution in Article I, Section 9.

20. Ian Ayres, *Super Crunchers: Why Thinking-by-Numbers Is the New Way to Be Smart* (New York: Bantam Books, 2007), pp. 2–3, 6; Mark Strauss, "The Grapes of Math," *Discover*, January 1991, pp. 50–51; Jay Palmer, "Grape Expectations," *Barron's*, December 30, 1996, pp. 17–19.

21. Robert Klitgaard, *Choosing Elites*, pp. 161–165.

22. Robert Klitgaard, *Elitism and Meritocracy in Developing Countries: Selection Policies for Higher Education* (Baltimore: The Johns Hopkins University Press, 1986), pp. 77–84.

23. Ibid., pp. 124, 147.

24. Malcolm Gladwell, *Outliers: The Story of Success* (New York: Little, Brown and Company, 2008), pp. 74, 112.

25. Richard H. Sander and Stuart Taylor, Jr., *Mismatch: How Affirmative Action Hurts Students It's Intended to Help, and Why Universities Won't Admit It* (New York: Basic Books, 2012), pp. 34, 59, 90–91, 146–147, 148, 150, 152, 154, 162, 231; Thomas Sowell, *Affirmative Action Around the World: An Empirical Study* (New Haven: Yale University Press, 2004), pp. 154–156.

26. Arthur Hu, "Minorities Need More Support," *The Tech* (M.I.T.), March 17, 1987, pp. 4, 6.

27. Richard H. Sander and Stuart Taylor, Jr., *Mismatch*, pp. 34–36.

28. Robin Wilson, "Article Critical of Black Students' Qualifications Roils Georgetown U. Law Center," *The Chronicle of Higher Education*, April 24, 1991, pp. A33, A35.

29. Richard H. Sander and Stuart Taylor, Jr., *Mismatch*, pp. 55–56, 231.

30. Philip E. Vernon, *Intelligence and Cultural Environment* (London: Methuen & Co., Ltd., 1969), p. 145.

31. Ibid., pp. 157–158.

32. Ibid., p. 168.

33. Mandel Sherman and Cora B. Key, "The Intelligence of Isolated Mountain Children," *Child Development*, Vol. 3, No. 4 (December 1932), p. 284.

34. Philip E. Vernon, *Intelligence and Cultural Environment*, p. 104.

35. Ibid., p. 101.

36. Ibid., p. 155.

37. Robert M. Yerkes, *Psychological Examining in the United States Army*, Memoirs of the National Academy of Sciences (Washington: Government Printing Office, 1921), Vol. 15, p. 705.

38. Arthur R. Jensen, "How Much Can We Boost IQ and Scholastic Achievement?" *Harvard Educational Review*, Winter 1969, p. 81.

39. H.H. Goddard, "The Binet Tests in Relation to Immigration," *Journal of Psycho-Asthenics*, Vol. 18, No. 2 (December 1913), p. 110.

40. William G. Bowen and Derek Bok, *The Shape of the River: Long-Term Consequences of Considering Race in College and University Admissions* (Princeton: Princeton University Press, 1998), p. 61. See also p. 259.

41. Bob Zelnick, *Backfire: A Reporter's Look at Affirmative Action* (Washington: Regnery Publishing, 1996), p. 132.

42. Robert Lerner and Althea K. Nagai, "Racial Preferences in Colorado Higher Education," Center for Equal Opportunity, pp. 6, 11.

43. William G. Bowen and Derek Bok, *The Shape of the River*, p. 21.

44. Stephan Thernstrom and Abigail Thernstrom, "Reflections on *The Shape of the River*," *UCLA Law Review*, Vol. 46, No. 5 (June 1999), p. 1589.

45. Arthur R. Jensen, "How Much Can We Boost IQ and Scholastic Achievement?" *Harvard Educational Review*, Winter 1969, p. 78.

46. Charles Murray, *Human Accomplishment: The Pursuit of Excellence in the Arts and Sciences, 800 B.C. to 1950* (New York: HarperCollins, 2003), p. 282.

47. Paul A. Witty and Martin D. Jenkins, "The Educational Achievement of a Group of Gifted Negro Children," *Journal of Educational Psychology*, Vol. 25, Issue 8 (November 1934), p. 593; Paul Witty and Viola Theman, "A Follow-up Study of Educational Attainment of Gifted Negroes," *Journal of Educational Psychology*, Vol. 34, Issue 1 (January 1943), pp. 35–47; Edelbert G. Rodgers, *The Relationship of Certain Measurable Factors in the Personal and Educational Backgrounds of Two Groups of Baltimore Negroes, Identified as*

Superior and Average in Intelligence as Fourth Grade Children, to their Educational, Social and Economic Achievement in Adulthood (Unpublished Doctoral Dissertation, New York University, 1956), University Microfilms, unpaged introduction and pp. 75–94.

48. Otto Klineberg, "Mental Testing of Racial and National Groups," *Scientific Aspects of the Race Problem*, edited by H.S. Jennings, et al (Washington: Catholic University Press, 1941), p. 282.

49. Rudolf Pintner, *Intelligence Testing: Methods and Results* (New York: Henry Holt and Company, 1923), p. 352; Clifford Kirkpatrick, *Intelligence and Immigration* (Baltimore: The Williams & Wilkins Company, 1926), pp. 24, 31, 34.

50. Philip E. Vernon, *Intelligence and Cultural Environment*, p. 155; Lester R. Wheeler, "A Comparative Study of the Intelligence of East Tennessee Mountain Children," *The Journal of Educational Psychology*, Vol. XXXIII, No. 5 (May 1942), pp. 322, 324.

51. Philip E. Vernon, *Intelligence and Cultural Environment*, p. 104.

52. Carl C. Brigham, *A Study of American Intelligence* (Princeton: Princeton University Press, 1923), p. xx.

53. Ibid., p. 110.

54. Carl C. Brigham, "Intelligence Tests of Immigrant Groups," *Psychological Review*, Vol. 37, Issue 2 (March 1930), p. 165.

55. Carl C. Brigham, *A Study of American Intelligence*, p. 29.

56. James R. Flynn, "The Mean IQ of Americans: Massive Gains 1932 to 1978," *Psychological Bulletin*, Vol. 95, No. 1, pp. 29–51; James R. Flynn, "Massive IQ Gains in 14 Nations: What IQ Tests Really Measure," *Psychological Bulletin*, Vol. 101, No. 2, pp. 171–191.

57. James R. Flynn, *Where Have All the Liberals Gone?: Race, Class, and Ideals in America* (Cambridge: Cambridge University Press, 2008), pp. 72–73, 87.

58. Ibid., pp. 110–111.

59. Ibid., pp. 89, 90.

60. Eric A. Hanushek, et al., "New Evidence About *Brown v. Board of Education*: The Complex Effects of School Racial Composition on Achievement," National Bureau of Economic Research, Working Paper 8741 (Cambridge, Massachusetts: National Bureau of Economic Research, 2002), Abstract.

61. See, for example, Paul Brest, "Some Comments on *Grutter v. Bollinger*," *Drake Law Review*, Vol. 51, p. 691; Gabriel J. Chin, "*Bakke* to the Wall: The Crisis of *Bakkean* Diversity," *William & Mary Bill of Rights Journal*, Vol. 4, No. 3 (1995–1996), pp. 888, 921–923; *Hopwood v. Texas Litigation Documents*, Part I, Volume 3, compiled by Kumar Percy (Buffalo, N.Y.: William S. Hein & Co., Inc., 2002), Document No. 57, "Deposition of Dean Paul Brest," pp. 32, 33–34, 35, 36, 38–39; *Hopwood v. Texas Litigation Documents*, Part I, Volume 3, compiled by Kumar Percy, Document No. 58, "Deposition of Lee Carroll Bollinger," pp. 35–36, 38–39; *Hopwood v. Texas Litigation Documents*, Part I, Volume 3, compiled by Kumar Percy, Document No. 60, "Oral Deposition of Judith Wegner," pp. 14–15.

62. Ellis B. Page and Timothy Z. Keith, "The Elephant in the Classroom: Ability Grouping and the Gifted," *Intellectual Talent: Psychometric and Social Issues*, edited by Camilla Persson Benbow and David Lubinski (Baltimore: The Johns Hopkins University Press, 1996), p. 208.

63. Edelbert G. Rodgers, *The Relationship of Certain Measurable Factors in the Personal and Educational Backgrounds of Two Groups of Baltimore Negroes, Identified as Superior and Average in Intelligence as Fourth Grade Children, to their Educational, Social and Economic Achievement in Adulthood* (Unpublished Doctoral Dissertation, New York University, 1956), University Microfilms, p. 50.

64. Stuart Buck, *Acting White: The Ironic Legacy of Desegregation* (New Haven: Yale University Press, 2010), pp. 11–17.

65. Theodore Dalrymple, *Life at the Bottom: The Worldview that Makes the Underclass* (Chicago: Ivan R. Dee, 2001), p. 69.

66. See Mary Gibson Hundley, *The Dunbar Story (1870–1955)* (New York: Vantage Press, 1965), p. 75.

67. Jervis Anderson, "A Very Special Monument," *The New Yorker*, March 20, 1978, p. 105.

68. Otto Klineberg, "Mental Testing of Racial and National Groups," *Scientific Aspects of the Race Problem*, edited by H.S. Jennings, et al., p. 280.

69. Arthur R. Jensen, "How Much Can We Boost IQ and Scholastic Achievement?" *Harvard Educational Review*, Winter 1969, pp. 86–87.

70. Clifford Kirkpatrick, *Intelligence and Immigration*, p. 31; Lester R. Wheeler, "A Comparative Study of the Intelligence of East Tennessee Mountain

Children," *The Journal of Educational Psychology*, Vol. XXXIII, No. 5 (May 1942), pp. 326–327.

71. H.J. Butcher, *Human Intelligence: Its Nature and Assessment* (New York: Harper & Row, 1968), p. 252.

72. Alexis de Tocqueville, *Democracy in America* (New York: Alfred A. Knopf, 1966), Vol. I, p. 365; Frederick Law Olmsted, *The Cotton Kingdom: A Traveller's Observations on Cotton and Slavery in the American Slave States*, edited by Arthur M. Schlesinger (New York: Modern Library, 1969), pp. 476n, 614–622; Hinton Rowan Helper, *The Impending Crisis of the South: How to Meet It*, enlarged edition (New York: A. B. Burdick, 1860), p. 34; Gunnar Myrdal, *An American Dilemma: The Negro Problem and Modern Democracy* (New York: Harper & Brothers, 1944), p. 70n.

73. David Hackett Fischer, *Albion's Seed: Four British Folkways in America* (Oxford: Oxford University Press, 1989), pp. 31–36, 72–77, 89–90, 120–121, 130–134, 233, 236–240, 252, 256–261, 284–285, 298, 303, 344–349, 368, 618–639, 674–675, 680–681, 703–708, 721–723. See also Grady McWhiney, *Cracker Culture: Celtic Ways in the Old South* (Tuscaloosa: University of Alabama Press, 1988), pp. 16–18.

74. Gunnar Myrdal, *An American Dilemma*, p. 70n.

75. Paul A. Witty and Martin D. Jenkins, "The Educational Achievement of a Group of Gifted Negro Children," *Journal of Educational Psychology*, Vol. 25, Issue 8 (November 1934), p. 593; Paul Witty and Viola Theman, "A Follow-up Study of Educational Attainment of Gifted Negroes," *Journal of Educational Psychology*, Vol. 34, Issue 1 (January 1943), p. 43; Edelbert G. Rodgers, *The Relationship of Certain Measurable Factors in the Personal and Educational Backgrounds of Two Groups of Baltimore Negroes, Identified as Superior and Average in Intelligence as Fourth Grade Children, to their Educational, Social and Economic Achievement in Adulthood* (Unpublished Doctoral Dissertation, New York University, 1956), University Microfilms, unpaged introduction and pp. 75–94.

76. Sandra Scarr and Richard A. Weinberg, "IQ Test Performance of Black Children Adopted by White Families," *American Psychologist*, October 1976, p. 731.

77. See, for example, Leonard Covello, *The Social Background of the Italo-American School Child* (Totowa, N.J.: Rowman and Littlefield, 1972), pp. 241–261; Charles Murray, *Human Accomplishment*, p. 291; Richard Gambino, *Blood of My Blood: The Dilemma of the Italian-Americans* (Garden City, N.Y.: Doubleday & Co., 1974), p. 225.

78. Thomas Sowell, "Assumptions versus History in Ethnic Education," *Teachers College Record*, Volume 83, Number 1 (Fall 1981), pp. 43–45.

79. Ibid., p. 45.

80. Kathryn G. Caird, "A Note on the Progress of Preference Students in First Year Accounting Courses," internal memorandum, University of Auckland (undated but probably 1989).

81. Patricia Cohen, "'Culture of Poverty' Makes a Comeback," *New York Times*, October 18, 2010, pp. A1 ff.

82. Richard J. Herrnstein and Charles Murray, *The Bell Curve*, p. 298.

83. Daniel Schwekendiek, "Height and Weight Differences Between North and South Korea," *Journal of Biosocial Science*, Vol. 41, No. 1 (January 2009), pp. 51–55. *The Economist* reported that North Koreans were "on average three inches shorter" than South Koreans. "We Need to Talk About Kim," *The Economist*, December 31, 2011, p. 8.

84. Richard J. Herrnstein and Charles Murray, *The Bell Curve*, p. 309.

85. Ibid., p. 304.

86. Ibid., p. 311.

87. Ibid., p. 310.

88. Ibid., p. 314.

89. John B. Judis, "Hearts of Darkness," *The Bell Curve Wars: Race, Intelligence, and the Future of America*, edited by Steven Fraser (New York: Basic Books, 1995), pp. 126–127, 128.

90. Michael Lind, "Brave New Right," Ibid., pp. 172, 174.

91. Steven Fraser, "Introduction," Ibid., p. 1.

92. Randall Kennedy, "The Phony War," Ibid., p. 182.

93. Stephen Jay Gould, "Curveball," Ibid., pp. 11, 20.

94. Henry Louis Gates, Jr., "Why Now?" Ibid., pp. 95–96. As a matter of fact, *The Bell Curve* does not say that environment plays no role. Moreover, the word "dismissal" implies not simply a rejection but a rejection without

consideration. Nevertheless, even when a proposition is rejected after extensive examination and consideration, the word "dismissal" is often used by those more interested in its propaganda effect than with its accuracy.

95. Nathan Glazer, "Scientific Truth and the American Dilemma," Ibid., p. 141.

96. Ibid., p. 147.

Chapter 6: Liberalism and Multiculturalism

1. Paul Hollander, *Anti-Americanism: Critiques at Home and Abroad 1965–1990* (New York: Oxford University Press, 1992), p. 455.

2. See, for example, Richard Lynn, "The Intelligence of American Jews," *Personality and Individual Differences*, Vol. 36, No. 1 (January 2004), p. 204; Richard Lynn and David Longley, "On the High Intelligence and Cognitive Achievements of Jews in Britain," *Intelligence*, Vol. 34, No. 6 (November-December 2006), p. 542.

3. Matthew Pratt Guterl, *The Color of Race in America 1900–1940* (Cambridge, Mass.: Harvard University Press, 2001), p. 67.

4. "The Passing of the Nordic Myth," *The Christian Century*, June 16, 1937, p. 765.

5. Franz Samelson, "From 'Race Psychology' to 'Studies in Prejudice': Some Observations on the Thematic Reversal in Social Psychology," *Journal of the History of the Behavioral Sciences*, Vol. 14 (1978), p. 268.

6. Otto Klineberg, "Mental Testing of Racial and National Groups," *Scientific Aspects of the Race Problem*, edited by H.S. Jennings, et al (Washington: Catholic University Press, 1941), p. 284.

7. Gunnar Myrdal, *An American Dilemma: The Negro Problem and Modern Democracy* (New York: Harper & Brothers, 1944), p. li. Within the main body of the book itself, this premise was explicitly repeated— "The Negro problem is primarily a white man's problem" (p. 669)— as well as being implicit in the whole approach taken.

8. Ibid., p. xlvii.

9. David W. Southern, *Gunnar Myrdal and Black-White Relations* (Baton Rouge: Louisiana State University Press, 1987), p. 74.

10. Alfred W. Blumrosen, *Black Employment and the Law* (New Brunswick: Rutgers University Press, 1971), p. vii.

11. James Baldwin, "Fifth Avenue, Uptown," *Esquire*, July 1960, pp. 73, 76.

12. Theodore Dalrymple, *Life at the Bottom: The Worldview That Makes the Underclass* (Chicago: Ivan R. Dee, 2001), p. 150.

13. Whitney M. Young, "The High Cost of Discrimination," *Ebony*, August 1965, p. 51.

14. Paul Johnson, *Enemies of Society* (New York: Atheneum, 1977), p. 237.

15. Kenneth Clark, "Behind the Harlem Riots— Two Views," *New York Herald Tribune*, July 20, 1964, pp. 1, 7.

16. Newton Garver, "What Violence Is," *The Nation*, June 24, 1968, pp. 821, 822.

17. National Committee of Negro Churchmen, "'Black Power,'" *New York Times*, July 31, 1966, p. E5.

18. Louis Harris, "U.S. Riots: Negroes, Whites Offer Views," *Los Angeles Times*, August 14, 1967, p. A5.

19. Frank Clifford and David Farrell, "L.A. Strongly Condemns King Verdicts, Riots," *Los Angeles Times*, May 6, 1992, pp. A1, A4.

20. "The Hard-Core Ghetto Mood," *Newsweek*, August 21, 1967, pp. 20, 21.

21. Ibid., p. 20.

22. Stephan Thernstrom and Abigail Thernstrom, *America in Black and White: One Nation, Indivisible* (New York: Simon & Schuster, 1997), p. 162.

23. Donald L. Horowitz, *Ethnic Groups in Conflict* (Berkeley: University of California Press, 1985), pp. 170–181; Robert A. Wilson and Bill Hosokawa, *East to America: A History of the Japanese in the United States* (New York: William Morrow, 1980), p. 123.

24. Mahathir bin Mohamad, *The Malay Dilemma* (Singapore: Asia Pacific Press, 1970), p. 25.

25. Myron Weiner, *Sons of the Soil: Migration and Ethnic Conflict in India* (Princeton: Princeton University Press, 1978), p. 250.

26. John A. A. Ayoade, "Ethnic Management of the 1979 Nigerian Constitution," *Canadian Review of Studies in Nationalism*, Spring 1987, p. 127.

27. "America Can't Be Colorblind Yet," *New York Times*, June 10, 1981, p. A30.

28. U.S. Bureau of the Census, *Historical Statistics of the United States: Colonial Times to 1957* (Washington, D.C.: U.S. Government Printing Office, 1960), p. 72.

29. Richard Vedder and Lowell Galloway, "Declining Black Employment," *Society*, July-August 1993, p. 57.

30. Walter Williams, *Race & Economics: How Much Can Be Blamed on Discrimination?* (Stanford: Hoover Institution Press, 2011), p. 42.

31. Ibid.

32. Ibid., pp. 33–34.

33. Charles H. Young and Helen R.Y. Reid, *The Japanese Canadians* (Toronto: University of Toronto Press, 1938), p. 49; Merle Lipton, *Capitalism and Apartheid: South Africa, 1910–84* (Totowa, New Jersey: Rowman & Allanheld, 1985), pp. 19–20; George M. Fredrickson, *White Supremacy: A Comparative Study in American and South African History* (New York: Oxford University Press, 1981), p. 233.

34. "A Divided Self: A Survey of France," *The Economist*, November 16, 2002, p. 11; Holman W. Jenkins, Jr., "Shall We Eat Our Young?" *Wall Street Journal*, January 19, 2005, p. A13; Nelson D. Schwartz, "Young, Down and Out in Europe," *New York Times*, January 1, 2010, pp. B1, B4.

35. See, for example, Gilbert Osofsky, *Harlem: The Making of a Ghetto* (New York: Harper and Row, 1966), p. 12; David Katzman, *Before the Ghetto: Black Detroit in the Nineteenth Century* (Urbana, IL: University of Illinois Press, 1973), pp. 35, 37, 102, 138, 139, 160; W.E.B. Du Bois, *The Philadelphia Negro: A Social Study* (New York: Schocken Books, 1967), p. 7; Constance McLaughlin Green, *The Secret City: A History of Race Relations in the Nation's Capital* (Princeton: Princeton University Press, 1967), p. 127; St. Clair Drake and Horace R. Cayton, *Black Metropolis: A Study of Negro Life in a Northern City* (New York: Harper & Row, 1962), Vol. I, pp. 44–45, 176n; Allan H. Spear, *Black Chicago: The Making of a Negro Ghetto, 1890–1920* (Chicago: University of Chicago Press, 1970), Chapter 1; Reynolds Farley, et al., *Detroit Divided* (New York: Russell Sage Foundation, 2000), pp. 145–146; Oliver Zunz, *The Changing Face of Inequality: Urbanization, Industrial Development, and Immigrants in Detroit, 1880–1920* (Chicago: University of Chicago Press, 1982), p. 353; Willard B. Gatewood, *Aristocrats of Color: The Black Elite, 1880–1920* (Bloomington: Indiana University Press, 1990), pp. 119, 125.

36. W.E.B. Du Bois, *The Philadelphia Negro*, pp. 41–42, 305–306.

37. Jacob Riis, *How the Other Half Lives: Studies among the Tenements of New York* (Cambridge, Mass.: Harvard University Press, 1970), p. 99; David Katzman, *Before the Ghetto*, pp. 35, 37, 102, 138, 139, 160; St. Clair Drake and Horace

R. Cayton, *Black Metropolis*, Vol. I, pp. 44–45; Willard B. Gatewood, *Aristocrats of Color*, pp. 119, 125.

38. Edward Glaeser and Jacob Vigdor, "The End of The Segregated Century: Racial Separation in America's Neighborhoods, 1890–2010," *Civic Report*, No. 66 (January 2012), pp. 3–4.

39. David Katzman, *Before the Ghetto*, pp. 35, 37, 102, 138, 139, 160; St. Clair Drake and Horace R. Cayton, *Black Metropolis*, Vol. I, pp. 44–45.

40. Oscar Handlin, *The Newcomers: Negroes and Puerto Ricans in a Changing Metropolis* (New York: Anchor Books, 1962), p. 46.

41. Jacob Riis, *How the Other Half Lives*, p. 99.

42. W.E.B. Du Bois, *The Philadelphia Negro*, pp. 33–36, 119–121.

43. E. Franklin Frazier, *The Negro in the United States*, revised edition (New York: The Macmillan Company, 1957), p. 405.

44. St. Clair Drake and Horace R. Cayton, *Black Metropolis*, Vol. I, p. 176n. See also Allan H. Spear, *Black Chicago*, Chapter 1.

45. See the title article in my *Black Rednecks and White Liberals* (San Francisco: Encounter Books, 2005).

46. W.E.B. Du Bois, *The Black North in 1901: A Social Study* (New York: Arno Press, 1969), p. 39.

47. Gilbert Osofsky, *Harlem*, pp. 43–44.

48. E. Franklin Frazier, *The Negro in the United States*, revised edition, p. 643.

49. Ibid., p. 630.

50. Gunnar Myrdal, *An American Dilemma*, p. 965.

51. See, for example, Willard B. Gatewood, *Aristocrats of Color*, pp. 186–187, 332; Allan H. Spear, *Black Chicago*, p. 168; E. Franklin Frazier, *The Negro in the United States*, revised edition, pp. 284–285; Florette Henri, *Black Migration: Movement North, 1900–1920* (Garden City, New York: Anchor Press, 1975), pp. 96–97; Gilbert Osofsky, *Harlem*, pp. 43–44; Ivan H. Light, *Ethnic Enterprise in America* (Berkeley: University of California Press, 1972), Figure 1 (after p. 100); W.E.B. Du Bois, *The Black North in 1901*, p. 25.

52. Willard B. Gatewood, *Aristocrats of Color*, pp. 65, 250; E. Franklin Frazier, *The Negro in the United States*, revised edition, pp. 250–251, 441; Davison M. Douglas, *Jim Crow Moves North: The Battle over Northern School Segregation, 1865–1954* (Cambridge: Cambridge University Press, 2005), pp. 137–153.

53. Douglas Henry Daniels, *Pioneer Urbanites: A Social and Cultural History of Black San Francisco* (Philadelphia: Temple University Press, 1980), pp. 171–173; E. Franklin Frazier, *The Negro in the United States*, revised edition, pp. 270–271.

54. See, for example, Isabel Wilkerson, *The Warmth of Other Suns: The Epic Story of America's Great Migration* (New York: Random House, 2010), p. 291; Irving Howe, *World of Our Fathers* (New York: Harcourt Brace Jovanovich, 1976), pp. 229–230.

55. Irving Howe, *World of Our Fathers*, pp. 229, 230. Similar patterns existed in Australia in the 1930s. Hilary Rubinstein, *Chosen: The Jews in Australia* (Sydney: Allen & Unwin, 1987), p. 177.

56. Isabel Wilkerson, *The Warmth of Other Suns*, p. 291.

57. Michael Tobias, "Dialectical Dreaming: The Western Perception of Mountain People," *Mountain People*, edited by Michael Tobias (Norman: University of Oklahoma Press, 1986), p. 191.

58. James M. McPherson, "Deconstructing Affirmative Action," *Perspectives* (American Historical Association), April 2003, online edition.

59. Ibid.

60. *United Steelworkers of America, AFL-CIO-CLC v. Weber*, 443 U.S. (1979), at 212.

61. *Regents of the University of California v. Bakke*, 438 U.S. (1978), at 265, 365–366.

62. Ibid., at 374 n.58.

Chapter 7: Race and Cosmic Justice

1. Andrew Hacker, *Two Nations: Black and White, Separate, Hostile, Unequal* (New York: Charles Scribner's Sons, 1992), p. 53.

2. Ibid., pp. xi, 19, 27.

3. Ibid., p. 29.

4. Ibid., p. 51.

5. Ibid., p. 23.

6. Gunnar Myrdal, *An American Dilemma: The Negro Problem and Modern Democracy* (New York: Harper & Brothers 1944), p. 964.

7. Tom Wicker, "The Worst Fear," *New York Times*, April 28, 1989, p. A39.

8. Susannah Meadows and Evan Thomas, "What Happened At Duke?" *Newsweek*, May 1, 2006, p. 51.

9.   Meg Jones, "Flynn Calls Looting, Beatings in Riverwest Barbaric," *Milwaukee Journal Sentinel*, July 6, 2011, pp. A1 ff.

10. See, for example, Ian Urbina, "Mobs Are Born as Word Grows By Text Message," *New York Times*, March 25, 2010, p. A1; Kirk Mitchell, "Attacks Change Lives on All Sides," *Denver Post*, December 6, 2009, pp. A1 ff; Alan Gathright, 7News Content Producer, "Black Gangs Vented Hatred for Whites in Downtown Attacks," *The DenverChannel.com*, December 5, 2009; Meg Jones, "Flynn Calls Looting, Beatings in Riverwest Barbaric," *Milwaukee Journal Sentinel*, July 6, 2011, pp. A1 ff; Mareesa Nicosia, "Four Skidmore College Students Charged in Assault; One Charged with Felony Hate Crime," *The Saratogian* (online), December 22, 2010; "Concealing Black Hate Crimes," *Investor's Business Daily*, August 15, 2011, p. A16; Joseph A. Slobodzian, "West Philly Man Pleads Guilty to 'Flash Mob' Assault," *Philadelphia Inquirer*, June 21, 2011, pp. B1 ff; Alfred Lubrano, "What's Behind 'Flash Mobs'?" *Philadelphia Inquirer*, March 28, 2010, pp. A1 ff; Stephanie Farr, "'Geezer' Won't Let Thugs Ruin His Walks," *Philadelphia Daily News*, October 20, 2011, Local section, p. 26; Barry Paddock and John Lauinger, "Subway Gang Attack," *New York Daily News*, July 18, 2011, News, p. 3.

11. Steve Chapman, "Race and the 'Flash Mob' Attacks," *Chicago Tribune*, June 8, 2011 (online).

12. Daniel J. Losen, Executive Summary, "Discipline Policies, Successful Schools, and Racial Justice," National Education Policy Center, School of Education, University of Colorado Boulder, October 2011.

13. David D. Cole, "Can Our Shameful Prisons Be Reformed?" *New York Review of Books*, November 19, 2009, p. 41.

14. Ibid.

15. Ibid.

16. Ibid.

17. See, for example, Theodore Dalrymple, *Life at the Bottom: The Worldview That Makes the Underclass* (Chicago: Ivan R. Dee, 2001), p. 69.

18. "Historical Poverty Tables: Table 4," U.S. Bureau of the Census, Current Population Survey, Annual Social and Economic Supplements. Downloaded June 29, 2007 from:
http://www.census.govhhes/www/poverty/histpov/hstpov4.html.

19. Martin A. Klein, "Introduction," *Breaking the Chains: Slavery, Bondage, and Emancipation in Modern Africa and Asia*, edited by Martin A. Klein (Madison: University of Wisconsin Press, 1993), pp. 19, 20. As of 1840, there were still more slaves in India than those emancipated by the British in the Caribbean. David Brion Davis, *The Problem of Slavery in the Age of Revolution 1770–1823* (Ithaca: Cornell University Press, 1975), p. 63.

20. Martin A. Klein, "Introduction," *Breaking the Chains*, edited by Martin A. Klein, p. 8.

21. Ibid., p. 11.

22. John Stuart Mill, "Considerations on Representative Government," *Collected Works of John Stuart Mill*, Vol. XIX: *Essays on Politics and Society*, edited by J.M. Robson (Toronto: University of Toronto Press, 1977), p. 395.

23. Abraham Lincoln to Albert G. Hodges, April 4, 1864, reprinted in *The Collected Works of Abraham Lincoln*, edited by Roy P. Basler (New Brunswick: Rutgers University Press, 1953), Vol. VII, p. 281.

24. Kevin Bales, "The Social Psychology of Modern Slavery," *Scientific American*, April 2002, pp. 80–88.

25. Orlando Patterson, *Slavery and Social Death: A Comparative Study* (Cambridge, Mass.: Harvard University Press, 1982), pp. 406–407; W. Montgomery Watt, *The Influence of Islam on Medieval Europe* (Edinburgh: Edinburgh University Press, 1972), p. 19; Bernard Lewis, *Race and Slavery in the Middle East: An Historical Enquiry* (New York: Oxford University Press, 1990), p. 11; Daniel Evans, "Slave Coast of Europe," *Slavery & Abolition*, Vol. 6, Number 1 (May 1985), p. 53, note 3; William D. Phillips, Jr., *Slavery from Roman Times to the Early Transatlantic Trade* (Minneapolis: University of Minnesota Press, 1985), p. 57.

26. Robert C. Davis, *Christian Slaves, Muslim Masters: White Slavery in the Mediterranean, the Barbary Coast, and Italy, 1500–1800* (New York: Palgrave Macmillan, 2003), p. 23; Philip D. Curtin, *The Atlantic Slave Trade: A Census* (Madison: University of Wisconsin Press, 1969), pp. 72, 75, 87.

27. Daniel J. Boorstin, *The Americans*, Vol. II: *The National Experience* (New York: Random House, 1965), p. 203.

28. Alexis de Tocqueville, *Democracy in America* (New York: Alfred A. Knopf, 1966), Vol. I, p. 365; Frederick Law Olmsted, *The Cotton Kingdom: A Traveller's*

Observations on Cotton and Slavery in the American Slave States, edited by Arthur M. Schlesinger (New York: Modern Library, 1969), pp. 476n, 614–622; Hinton Rowan Helper, *The Impending Crisis of the South: How to Meet It*, enlarged edition (New York: A. B. Burdick, 1860), p. 34.

29. David Hackett Fischer, *Albion's Seed: Four British Folkways in America* (Oxford: Oxford University Press, 1989), pp. 31–33, 89–91, 130–134, 252, 284–285, 298, 303, 345–346, 365–368, 621–630, 674–675, 680–682, 703–708, 721–723.

30. Herbert G. Gutman, *The Black Family in Slavery and Freedom, 1750–1925* (New York: Vintage Press, 1977), pp. 32, 45; Leon F. Litwack, *Been in the Storm So Long* (New York: Alfred A. Knopf, 1979), p. 238.

31. Stephan Thernstrom and Abigail Thernstrom, *America in Black and White: One Nation, Indivisible* (New York: Simon and Schuster, 1997), p. 238.

32. Henry A. Walker, "Black-White Differences in Marriage and Family Patterns," *Feminism, Children and the New Families*, edited by Sanford M. Dornbusch and Myra H. Strober (New York: The Guilford Press, 1988), p. 92.

33. U.S. Bureau of the Census, *Historical Statistics of the United States: Colonial Times to 1957* (Washington, D.C.: U.S. Government Printing Office, 1960), p. 72.

Chapter 8: The Past and The Future

1. Madison Grant, *The Passing of the Great Race or the Racial Basis of European History,* revised edition (New York: Charles Scribner's Sons, 1918), p. 100.

2. Gunnar Myrdal, *An American Dilemma: The Negro Problem and Modern Democracy* (New York: Harper & Brothers, 1944), pp. xlvii, 669.

3. Charles Murray, *Losing Ground: American Social Policy, 1950–1980* (New York: Basic Books, 1984), pp. 116–117.

4. Theodore Dalrymple, *Life at the Bottom: The Worldview That Makes the Underclass* (Chicago: Ivan R. Dee, 2001), pp. 69, 70.

5. Stephan Thernstrom and Abigail Thernstrom, *America in Black and White: One Nation, Indivisible* (New York: Simon & Schuster, 1997), p. 233.

6. Thomas Sowell, *Affirmative Action Around the World: An Empirical Study* (New Haven: Yale University Press, 2004), pp. 19–20.

7.   For detailed examples, see chapter 1 of my *Affirmative Action Around the World*.

8.   Gordon P. Means, "Ethnic Preference Policies in Malaysia," *Ethnic Preference and Public Policy in Developing States*, edited by Neil Nevitte and Charles H. Kennedy (Boulder: Lynne Rienner Publishers, Inc., 1986), p. 108; V. K. Natraj, "Reservation and the OBCs," *The Hindu* (India), April 4, 2000.

9.   Gardiner Harris, "With Affirmative Action, India's Rich Gain School Slots Meant for Poor," *New York Times*, October 8, 2012, p. A4. See also Marc Galanter, *Competing Equalities: Law and the Backward Classes in India* (Berkeley: University of California Press, 1984), p. 469.

10. Ozay Mehmet and Yip Yat Hoong, "An Empirical Evaluation of Government Scholarship Policy in Malaysia," *Higher Education* (The Netherlands), Vol. 14, No. 2 (April 1985), p. 202.

11. Sara Rimer and Karen W. Arenson, "Top Colleges Take More Blacks, but Which Ones?" *New York Times*, June 24, 2004, pp. A1, A18.

12. Richard H. Sander and Stuart Taylor, Jr., *Mismatch: How Affirmative Action Hurts Students It's Intended to Help, and Why Universities Won't Admit It* (New York: Basic Books, 2012), p. 152. See also p. 154.

13. Ibid., p. 138.

14. Ibid., p. 154.

15. Ibid., pp. 34, 55–56, 59, 90–91, 146–147, 148, 150, 152, 154, 162, 231; Thomas Sowell, *Affirmative Action Around the World*, pp. 154–156.

16. Richard H. Sander and Stuart Taylor, Jr., *Mismatch*, p. 61.

17. Walter E. Williams, *The State Against Blacks* (New York: McGraw-Hill, 1982), p. 31.

18. *Equal Employment Opportunity Commission v. Sears, Roebuck & Company*, 839 F.2d 302 at 311, 360; Peter Brimelow, "Spiral of Silence," *Forbes*, May 25, 1992, p. 77.

19. The Civil Rights Act of 1991 (Public Law 102–166 [S. 1745]).

20. See, for example, John Herbers, "Local Pressure Bringing More Lending in Inner Cities," *New York Times*, May 5, 1986, p. B11; William Claiborne, "Jackson's Fundraising Methods Spur Questions," *Washington Post*, March 27, 2001, pp. A1 ff; "Fannie Mae's Political Immunity," *Wall Street Journal*, July 29, 2008, p. A16; Kenneth R. Timmerman, "Freddie Mac, Verizon Made

Jesse's Hit List," *Insight on the News*, May 27, 2002, pp. 20–21; Peter Schweizer, *Architects of Ruin: How Big Government Liberals Wrecked the Global Economy—and How They Will Do It Again If No One Stops Them* (New York: Harper Collins, 2009), p. 14.

21. Paul Craig Roberts, "How to Rob A Bank Legally," *Washington Times*, December 20, 1993, p. A24.

22. Joint Center for Housing Studies, Harvard University, "The 25th Anniversary of the Community Reinvestment Act: Access to Capital in an Evolving Financial Services System," March 2002, p. 125.

23. Antoine-Nicolas de Condorcet, *Sketch for a Historical Picture of the Progress of the Human Mind*, translated by June Barraclough (London: Weidenfeld and Nicolson, 1955), p. 174; John Rawls, *A Theory of Justice* (Cambridge, Massachusetts: Harvard University Press, 1971), p. 100.

INDEX

Abstract People (see also Intertemporal Abstractions), 19, 50, 89, 101, 104, 105, 118

Academia, 2–3, 10, 14–15, 40, 136

Acculturation, 98–102, 103, 111

Achievement versus Privilege, 52–53

Affirmative Action, 104, 128, 129–131

Africa, 11–12, 119, 121

Age, 16, 75, 77

Alcohol, 10, 18, 51

American Economic Association, 31, 33, 34, 35

An American Dilemma, 88, 89, 100, 102, 111, 168 (note 7)

Angels, 19, 53, 80–81, 108, 109, 111, 121, 123

Anglo-Saxons, 1, 21, 23, 39

Argentina, 8, 9, 15, 106

Arguments without Arguments, 94, 104, 106, 115

Armenians, 8, 14, 89

Asian Americans, 4–5, 6, 53, 54, 64–65, 68, 76, 104, 128n, 131

Australia, 9, 12, 15, 23, 32, 86, 172 (note 55)

Baldwin, James, 90, 91

Balkans, 9, 14, 15, 90

Baltics, 13, 14, 15, 90

Banks, 5, 9, 135–136

Bar Examinations, 67, 131

The Bell Curve, 81–84, 167 (note 94)

Blacks, 3, 4–6, 26, 27, 30, 31, 35, 37–38, 64, 65–66, 68, 87, 89, 109

acculturation: 98–100, 101–102, 103

"acting white": 76, 110

black crime: 111–118, 123, 126

black families: 62, 63, 116, 120–121, 126

black IQs: 25, 71–72, 74, 75, 76, 77, 78–79, 80, 82

black labor force participation: 95, 120

black migrations: 24, 98, 99–100, 101, 111

black orphans adopted by white families: 79

black public opinion: 92–93, 102

black residential patterns: 20

black soldiers in the First World War: 68, 72–73

black students: 65–67, 69–70

black subculture: 75–79

black unemployment: 93, 95–96

black violence: 53, 103, 123

black-white comparisons: 4, 5–6, 13, 19, 24, 25, 26, 37, 38, 61, 63, 64, 65–67, 68, 70, 71, 74, 75, 76, 77, 78, 80, 82, 88, 89, 90, 91, 93, 95–96, 98, 112, 114, 116–117, 119, 120, 123, 124–125, 126

black youths: 95, 112, 113–114, 115, 123, 127

Ely, Richard T., 31–32, 33, 34–35

Environment

   cultural legacy: 108

   immediate surroundings: 79–80, 88, 108

   versus heredity: 81–82, 88

Equality, 137–139

Eugenics, 23, 26, 27, 32–33, 60–61, 73, 122

Europe, 10–14, 15, 23, 24, 25, 26, 27, 28, 29, 30–31, 36, 37, 41, 43, 46, 47, 49, 50, 86, 87, 96, 100, 101, 105, 118, 124–125, 127

   Eastern Europe: 13–14, 15, 26, 29, 30, 36, 37, 100, 101, 125

   Europeans: 8, 11, 13, 14, 19, 20, 21, 23, 25, 27, 36, 41, 77, 101, 119, 121

   Northern Europe: 19, 30, 31, 41

   Southern Europe: 24, 29, 30, 31, 37, 43

Evidence, 82–83, 95, 104, 113, 115

Ex ante versus *Ex post*, 52

Exploitation, 51–52

External Factors (see also Internal Factors), 15, 20, 58, 115, 116, 127

Fair Labor Standards Act, 22–23, 59, 61, 63

False Dichotomy, 124–125

First World War, 24, 25, 49, 57, 68, 72, 73n, 77, 78, 85n, 86, 87

Flynn, James R., 64, 74, 75, 77, 82, 85n

France, 7, 37, 57, 59

Frazier, E. Franklin, 3, 20

"Free Persons of Color," 42–43

Freedom, 31–32, 38, 88, 136

Galton, Francis, 22–23, 59, 61, 63

Genes, 7, 14, 41, 43, 65, 68, 77, 82, 122

Genetic Determinism, 15, 22–24, 33, 60, 71, 81, 84, 88, 94, 122, 124, 136

Geography, 10–15, 16, 56, 122, 125

Georgetown University, 67, 114

German Jews, 20, 49, 100, 101

Germans, 8, 14, 15, 18n, 30, 45–46, 49–50, 51, 101, 109

Germany, 2, 15, 16, 36, 37, 50, 75, 82

Grant, Madison, 21, 22, 24, 27–29, 35–36, 40–41, 43, 59, 61, 63, 72, 82, 87, 125, 136

Greeks, 8, 14, 25, 41, 43, 72

Habsburg Empire, 45, 49, 53

Hacker, Andrew, 108, 109

Handlin, Oscar, 13, 98

Harlem, 20, 90, 91, 103, 112

Harvard University, 32, 34, 40, 70, 84, 130

Hebrides Islands, 9, 67, 68, 72

Height, 57, 58, 59, 81

Heredity versus Environment, 81–82, 88

Herrnstein, Richard J., 81, 82–83, 84

Hitler, Adolf, 2, 27, 136

Holocaust, 2, 36, 87, 136

Horses, 10–11

Housing, 93

   housing projects: 90–91

   residential clustering: 19–20, 96–97, 98

Hume, David, 44, 50